bodyFiT

Beyond the Scale

The Ultimate 6-week Transformation Program

RHONA PARSONS

The Balance Coach

Every accomplishment starts with the decision to try.

Published by Ruby Blue Publishing.

For information, visit: www.rhonaparsons.com

Cover Design by Shine Creative: www.shine-creative.ca

Photos by Lori Jantz

First edition: June 2023

CONTENTS

WELCOME

Congratulations on taking the first step towards your goals and purchasing the bodyFIT Beyond The Scale Ultimate 6-week program!

bodyFIT is the program that will help you achieve the transformation you are looking for. With commitment, hard work, and belief that you can generate outstanding results, if you choose to use what you learn, you will ROCK THIS!

The bodyFIT program is achievable; all you have to do is follow the guidance in this book, be excited about change, and be accountable to yourself and even someone else. Of course, discipline, motivation, and patience are still all required. Research shows that if you share your goals with someone, you are more likely to achieve them.

Are you ready for your transformation? Set your GPS to your goals, and let's get started!

GOALS **+ P**LANS **= S**UCCESS

Here's to your success!

Alena

WHAT IS IN THE bodyFIT PROGRAM?

- A fantastic BONUS 2-week Re-set training guide. These first two weeks will guide you through fitness, health, and wellness regimes to prepare your body and mind for the 6-week program.

- Easy-to-follow instructions on figuring out what you are eating, choosing the right foods for optimal success, and daily tracking sheets for journalling your food.

- Posture, mobility, and flexibility assessments to help you learn more about your body and to know where you are starting from, taking into account any injuries or imbalances you may have in your body.

- A 6-week transformational program that will take you beyond the scale with fun and challenging workouts.

- An in-depth wellness program helping you prepare your mind for success, and to help you overcome any roadblocks you may come across.

RE-SET FOR bodyFIT

Duration: 2 weeks

- A nutritional training guide to help you get your eating on track

- Exercise suggestions to get you prepared for the bodyFIT program

- Mindset and wellness nourishment to help set you up for success over the next eight weeks.

The first two weeks will prepare you for the 6-week bodyFIT program by fueling your body with the right foods and helping you get into the right mindset. The information on the following pages will help you dive deeper into how to make the right choices over the next eight weeks. You will also learn how to be mentally and emotionally prepared for any roadblocks that may show up.

Let's get started!

1. Go to **GETACTIVEQUESTIONNAIRE_ENG.pdf (csep.ca)** and complete the GET ACTIVE Form before beginning the Re-set program. After completing this form, you will know you are ready for this program.

2. On the next page, you are going to figure out your BMR (basic metabolic rate) to see what your daily caloric intake should be.

3. Next, you will learn how to master reading a nutritional label. This information is vital in understanding how food can affect your weight and help you choose the right foods to succeed from the program's beginning.

4. You will record your food over the next three days. Writing down your eating will give you a clear picture of whether your eating needs tweaking to provide the proper fuel for the bodyFIT program.

5. Remember that these are guidelines only; knowledge is power. If you have a healthy eating plan that works for you, please continue to use it but take the time to write out your meals for the next three days so that you know your current eating plan will work for the bodyFIT program. These first two weeks will give you great insight into how you are fueling your body.

6. If you are not exercising, refer to page 22 for guidelines on starting an exercise regime to prepare your body for the bodyFIT program.

7. Getting into a great mindset will set you on the road to success. Beginning on page 23, use the information to help you on your journey.

HOW MANY CALORIES SHOULD YOU BE EATING?

You use energy no matter what you do, even when sleeping. The Basic Metabolic Rate (B.M.R. – the minimal number of calories your body burns if you stay in bed all day) uses the totals of your height, weight, age, and gender to calculate the number of calories you need to ingest to be at rest all day.

Eating less than your B.M.R. can put you into starvation mode (the body begins to reserve all foods coming in).

Go to the following website to calculate your B.M.R. and activity level:

www.calculator.net/bmr-calculator

Input the information required, and once you know your B.M.R., you will see information on the total calories needed when you apply the level of activity that you do.

E.g., The B.M.R. for a moderately active (daily exercise/intense exercise 3-4 times/week) 61-year-old woman who is 5'5" and weighs 140lbs:

BMR is 1201 kcals

Moderate Activity: add 660 kcals

Total Daily Calorie Needs: 1861 kcals.

According to the Dietary Guidelines for Americans, it is recommended that 500-750 fewer calories need to be ingested in a day to lose 1 to 1.5 lbs a week. Now, this doesn't mean that you eat below your B.M.R. No, it means that you need to burn 500 to 750 calories daily through physical exercise.

READING A NUTRITIONAL LABEL

Calories (cals) are how much energy is created from one serving of food. One of the best tools is the nutritional label. By learning to read a nutritional label, you will always know what you put in your mouth.

Reading a nutritional label will come naturally to you after a while. Practice by learning to read all the labels on the food containers you already have in your cupboards and fridge. I'm sure this will be a great eye-opener for you!

Here are the five fundamental formulas you need to know:

1-gram carbohydrate (cho) = 4 calories

1-gram protein   = 4 calories

1-gram fat   = 9 calories

4.5-grams sugar   = 1 teaspoon

*Sodium intake should not exceed 1500-2000 mg/day

Write the formulas down and take the list with you when you go grocery shopping so you can easily read the nutritional labels and make the right food choices as you buy the food.

> A great time-saving idea is to make time each weekend and prepare all your dinners for the following week.
>
> Food prep will set you up for success when you are hungry.

Note: If reading nutritional labels is new, know that this takes time and practice.

Here is a typical nutritional label. The calories are for a 1-cup serving.

		Nutrition Facts
		Servings Per Container 2
		Serving Size 1 cup (228g)

			% Daily Value*
Total calories:	*250	**Amount Per Serving**	
		Calories 250	
		Total Fat 12g	**18%**
Fat:	12g x 9 = 108 cals	Saturated Fat 3g	**15%**
		Trans Fat 3g	
		Cholesterol 30mg	**10%**
Sodium:	= 470 mg	**Sodium** 470mg	**20%**
Cho:	31g x 4 = 124 cals	**Total Carbohydrate** 31g	**10%**
		Dietary Fiber 0g	**0%**
Sugars:	= 5 g	Sugars 5g	
Protein:	5g x 4 = 20 cals	**Protein** 5g	

In summary, this food label shows that the food serving of 1 cup is approximately 43% fat, 49% cho, and only 8% protein. Keep in mind that this is only one food eaten during the day.

Writing down your food, calculating the nutritional value of each meal, and totaling the columns can keep you on track with the food you are ingesting.

Research shows that using the following daily percentages: approximately 20% fat, 30% protein, and 50% carbohydrates (cho) will keep you on track to success.

*Knowing right away that 1 gram of fat is higher than both protein and cho, you can quickly lower your caloric intake by choosing foods lower in fat.

RECORDING YOUR FOOD

The following two weeks will be a tremendous opportunity for you to figure out your eating plan for the 6-week bodyFIT program.

FOOD JOURNALLING

On the following page, you have an example of a day's worth of meals journalized and broken down into six columns: total calories, fat, carbohydrates (cho), protein, sodium, and sugar.

Over the next three days, on pages 16-18, you will record your daily food intake. Eat what you typically eat - don't change your eating habits because you need to see what and how much food you are fuelling your body with. This information will give you great insight into how you usually eat and if you need to change your eating habits for the next eight weeks.

If recording your food is unfamiliar to you, it will take a little time, but I promise you, the amount of information you will learn over the next three days will be worth it!

Record everything in grams – the conversion to calories happens at the bottom of the sheet. If you eat something with a food label on the container, eat the serving size shown and record that information on your sheet. Refer to the food label example on page 15 if you are unclear about what to record.

At the end of the day, total up the six individual columns. Next, multiply the number of grams by the number of calories for the fat, cho, and protein columns to get the total calories for each column. Then, individually, divide these three numbers by the total number of calories to get the percentage of each column. This information will give you the percentages of how much fat, cho, and protein you are eating. Record this information on page 19.

NUTRITIONAL JOURNALLING

EXAMPLE	TOTAL CALORIES	FAT (g)	CHO (g)	PROTEIN (g)	SODIUM (mg)	SUGARS (g)
BREAKFAST:						
¾C frozen blueberries	80	0	19	1	10	13
2C fresh spinach	20	0	3	2	80	0
One scoop of Protein powder (Isagenix)	118.5	2.5	12	12	85	5.5
2 cups water	0	0	0	0	0	0
Coffee	0	0	0	0	0	0
TOTAL:	**218.5 cals**	**2.5g**	**34g**	**15g**	**175mg**	**18.5g**
LUNCH:						
Multi-grain bun	205	5	34	6	410	2
One tsp mustard	0	0	0	0	0	0
½ tbsp. mayonnaise	20	2	.5	0	40	0
½ C roast chicken	176	4	0	35	84	0
½ C fresh spinach	5		.7	.5	20	0
½ tomato	16	0	3	1	4	2
1oz cheddar cheese	109	9	0	7	230	0
TOTAL:	**531 cals**	**20g**	**38.2g**	**49.5g**	**788mg**	**4g**
SNACK:						
Four dried prunes	100	0	24	1	0	15
TOTAL:	**100 cals**		**24g**	**1g**		**15g**
DINNER:						
½ lb teriyaki salmon	230	6	10	34	0	3
¾ C white sushi rice	177	1	39	3	5	0
Spinach salad	48	0	9	3		
One piece of dark chocolate	59	4	5	.75	9	4.5
TOTAL:	**514 cals**	**11g**	**63g**	**40.75g**	**14mg**	**7.5g**
SNACK:						
3 tbsp. hummus	90	6	6	3	65	0
Beet crackers (16)	135	7	16	2	50	1
Coffee	0	0	0	0	0	0
TOTAL:	**225 cals**	**13g**	**22g**	**5g**	**115mg**	**1g**
TOTALS:	1588.5 cals	46.5g x9 418.5 cal 1588.5	181.2g x4 724.8 cal 1588.5	111.25g x4 445 cal 1588.5	1092mg	46g
Divide by total calories =Total percentage of calories:		26%	46%	28%	1092 mg	46 g

*Use the following three sheets to help write your three-day eating journal.

NUTRITIONAL JOURNAL – DAY ONE

FOOD	TOTAL CALORIES	FAT (g)	CHO (g)	PROTEIN (g)	SODIUM - mg	SUGARS (g)
BREAKFAST:						
LUNCH:						
SNACK:						
DINNER:						
SNACK:						
TOTALS:		x9	x4	x4		

NUTRITIONAL JOURNAL - DAY TWO

FOOD	TOTAL CALORIES	FAT (g)	CHO (g)	PROTEIN (g)	SODIUM - mg	SUGARS (g)
BREAKFAST:						
LUNCH:						
SNACK:						
DINNER:						
SNACK:						
TOTALS:		x9	x4	x4		

NUTRITIONAL JOURNAL – DAY THREE

FOOD	TOTAL CALORIES	FAT (g)	CHO (g)	PROTEIN (g)	Sodium (mg)	Sugars (g)
BREAKFAST:						
LUNCH:						
SNACK:						
DINNER:						
SNACK:						
TOTALS:		x9	x4	x4		

TOTAL CALORIE AND PERCENTAGE RECORDINGS

DAY 1: TOTAL CALORIES: _____   CHANGES TO BE MADE:

Total Fat percentage: _____%   _____

Total cho percentage: _____%   _____

Total Protein percentage: _____%   _____

Total Sodium: _____mg   _____

Total Sugar: _____g   _____

DAY 2: TOTAL CALORIES: _____   CHANGES TO BE MADE:

Total Fat percentage: _____%   _____

Total cho percentage: _____%   _____

Total Protein percentage: _____%   _____

Total Sodium: _____mg   _____

Total Sugar: _____g   _____

DAY 3: TOTAL CALORIES: _____   CHANGES TO BE MADE:

Total Fat percentage: _____%   _____

Total cho percentage: _____%   _____

Total Protein percentage: _____%   _____

Total Sodium: _____mg   _____

Total Sugar: _____g   _____

MEAL EXAMPLES FOR RE-SET

Breakfast:

- Protein shake: 1 cup water, 1/3 cup Simply egg whites (pasteurized), 2 cups fresh spinach, 1/3 cup of berries (strawberries, blueberries, raspberries).

- Two eggs (poached or scrambled), one piece of rye, multigrain, or gluten-free toast, 1 tsp. Butter or plant-based butter.

- One cup light plain Greek yogurt, 1/3 cup of berries, ¼ cup granola.

- 1/3 cup uncooked oatmeal or your favourite grain, 1 cup water, and one apple cut into cubes. Once cooked (about 8 minutes), add ¼ cup egg whites, turn the setting to low and cook for 2 minutes, stirring continuously or until the egg whites are cooked).

- Avocado Toast - ½ avocado served on one piece rye, multigrain, or gluten-free toast, 1 tsp. Butter or plant-based butter.

Lunch and Dinners:

Make sure you have one protein with each meal. Examples:

- One serving of protein (chicken, turkey, fish, or shellfish)

- Two eggs

- ½ cup low-fat cottage cheese; plant-based eaters – quinoa

- ½ cup tofu, beans, chickpeas, etc.)

Eat all the veggies you want.

> Check out the table on page 55 to help you gauge the most appropriate amount for each food type.

SOME GREAT FOOD SUGGESTIONS

FOOD IS ONE OF LIFE'S PLEASURES...

PROTEIN	CARBOHYDRATES	FATS
Chicken/Turkey breast, skinless	Asparagus	Almond Butter
Chicken/Turkey breast, deli-style	Beans	Plant-based Butter
Veal	Broccoli	Almonds
Lean Lamb	Cabbage	Macadamia Nuts
Turkey bacon	Cauliflower	Flaxseeds
Egg whites	Kale	Walnuts
Egg beaters	Mushrooms	Avocado
Eggs	Zucchini	Canola Oil
Tofu	Squash	Coconut Oil
Beans	Alfalfa sprouts	Olive Oil
Fish/Seafood	Bean sprouts	Olives
Cottage cheese, low fat/dry	Celery	Salmon
Soft cheeses (feta, goat, ricotta, skim mozzarella)	Cucumber	Tuna
Protein powder	Hummus	Trout
Soy burgers, hot dogs, sausages	Lettuce	Atlantic/Pacific Mackerel
Skim milk	Salsa	
Plain yogurt	Spinach	
Quinoa	Tomato	
	Water chestnuts	
	Apples	
	Berries	
	Cherries	
	Cantaloupe	
	Grapes	
	Kiwi	
	Melon	
	Orange	
	Pear	
	Pineapple	
	Watermelon	
	Rolled oats	
	Rye, multigrain, or gluten-free bread	
	Low-fat and sugar-free granola	

"LET FOOD BE THY MEDICINE AND MEDICINE BE THY FOOD"
-HIPPOCRATES

EXERCISE GUIDELINES

FITNESS

If you already have a fitness routine, continue it for the next two weeks. If not, below is a guideline to help your body prepare for the bodyFIT program.

CARDIO

Begin by walking twenty to thirty minutes at a good pace five days per week. If you have some, use your walking poles, they are amazing! If twenty minutes seems like a lot, walk for 10 minutes, then turn around and return to where you began. It will only feel like a 10-minute walk. Check out the heart rate information on pages 57-60 to help you determine your target heart rate and learn about the Rate of Perceived Exertion scale (RPE).

WAIT TRAINING

I call this Wait Training because that's precisely what we need to do; wait for the muscles to let go and relax. Five to ten minutes a day of stretching and lengthening the body either after your workout or ½ hour before you go to bed, shown on pages 97 and 98.

MINDSET

Your mindset is the beliefs about yourself that can be positive or negative and must be exercised too. Your thoughts influence how you think, feel, and act in every situation. For you to achieve your upcoming goals, you need to be open to any possibilities that arise. Over the next eight weeks, setbacks or challenges may appear and need to be seen as opportunities for growth. With a great mindset, you will overcome any obstacles that show up on your path.

MINDSET NOURISHMENT

Upon waking every morning, try to create 30 minutes for yourself to help you set your day up for success. Even if you must break up the 30 minutes into three 10-minute sections, it'll help you get into practicing mindfulness – the practice of being present in any given moment. This is one of the keys to success!

Don't go on your phone. When we go on our phones and check our emails, we are already dealing with someone else's business. The start of the day should begin with your business.

Water: Begin with drinking two cups of warm water. Warming the water is to have it at your body's temperature so it is readily digestible. Your body has fasted the entire night, and the water will awaken your internal organs.

Breathwork: After drinking the warm water and making your favourite tea/coffee, find a quiet place to sit, and if you want to, find a lovely piece of relaxing music to play.

Close your eyes and begin focusing on your breath. Can you hear the words SO as you breathe in and HAM (pronounced HUM) as you breathe out? "SO HAM" means "I AM." These two words are the mantra of the breath and can help you stay present in each moment. Stay with your breath for 5-10 minutes, allowing the body to wake up and begin your day easily and gracefully.

Gratitude: *"Gratitude is the rich soil to start growing amazing things!"*

Gratitude is the next step to help you move toward your goals and begin your day positively. Being grateful for all you have is essential to living a healthy, stress-free life. The key is to feel the gratitude in your heart when thinking about what you are grateful for. Over the next 14 days, every morning, write down three things/persons/experiences you are thankful for on the sheets provided and <u>why</u> you are grateful. (Sheets begin on page 25.) Gratitude is one of the keys to manifestation.

Place the sheets somewhere to remind you what you are grateful for all day. Warmth and fuzziness should be the results you get. 🖤

You can also declare an affirmation for seeing your ideal future as it is happening right now. This is a great way to bring all you desire into your life. Continue to do this daily, and you will begin to see life a little differently.

Daily affirmation examples:

- I am healthy and strong
- I am confident in myself
- I am achieving the goals I have set
- I am amazing!
- Life is wonderful!

What affirmations ring true for you?

_____

_____

_____

Happiness: Before you begin your day, close your eyes, and ask, "How do I want to show up in the world today?". Notice the first word that comes to mind and take this word with you throughout your day. Smile at everyone you meet. It'll make you feel good; you never know whose life you will change with just your beautiful smile. Go and have a wonderful day. 🖤

*A more detailed wellness guide begins on page 77.

I AM HAPPY AND GRATEFUL FOR: DATE: _____

1._____

_____

2._____

_____

3._____

_____

I AM HAPPY AND GRATEFUL FOR: DATE: _____

1._____

_____

2._____

_____

3._____

_____

I AM HAPPY AND GRATEFUL FOR: DATE: _____

1._____

_____

2._____

_____

3._____

_____

I AM HAPPY AND GRATEFUL FOR: DATE: _____

1._____

_____

2._____

_____

3._____

_____

I AM HAPPY AND GRATEFUL FOR: DATE: _____

1._____

_____

2._____

_____

3._____

_____

I AM HAPPY AND GRATEFUL FOR: DATE: _____

1._____

_____

2._____

_____

3._____

_____

I AM HAPPY AND GRATEFUL FOR: DATE: _____

1._____

_____

2._____

_____

3._____

_____

I AM HAPPY AND GRATEFUL FOR: DATE: _____

1._____

_____

2._____

_____

3._____

_____

I AM HAPPY AND GRATEFUL FOR: DATE: _____

1._____

_____

2._____

_____

3._____

_____

I AM HAPPY AND GRATEFUL FOR: DATE: _____

1._____

_____

2._____

_____

3._____

_____

I AM HAPPY AND GRATEFUL FOR: DATE: _____

1._____

_____

2._____

_____

3._____

_____

I AM HAPPY AND GRATEFUL FOR: DATE: _____

1._____

_____

2._____

_____

3._____

_____

I AM HAPPY AND GRATEFUL FOR: DATE: _____

1._____

_____

2._____

_____

3._____

_____

I AM HAPPY AND GRATEFUL FOR: DATE: _____

1._____

_____

2._____

_____

3._____

_____

TESTIMONIAL:

My name is Joan, and I was 70 when I began the bodyFIT program in January 2021. I aimed to lose 25 pounds, tone my body, lose some inches, and generally feel better. The program came along when I was in a slump; I had gained weight and wasn't feeling as energetic as usual.

My coach was energetic, and her cheerful nature was always encouraging. Recording what I ate and drinking eight glasses of water daily helped keep me on track. I found I wasn't hungry and craving empty carbs like I normally would. I had my moments but usually managed to eat a healthier snack or protein rather than junk food.

The exercise sessions were great because they were short, and I always felt like I had a good workout. At the end of 6 weeks, I had lost 14.8 pounds and 21.5 inches! I gained other benefits from the program as well. I can now go up and down stairs one foot after the other instead of putting one foot on the step and pulling the other one after it. My arthritic knees are much stronger now, probably from strengthening the muscles. I notice my balance is better as well. Also, my right arm, which has a tear in the rotator cuff, is much more flexible, and I hope to avoid surgery. Although I can't do some weight exercises with my right arm, I feel the ones I can do strengthen it. As my coach always says, "Listen to your body." Although I am not watching my diet as closely and don't always drink my eight glasses of water, I am maintaining my weight loss and find I don't crave the bad carbs the way I used to. I feel great. Your hard work will pay off.

Joan Y. | BC Canada

YOU ARE WHAT YOU EAT

THE THREE PRIMARY NUTRIENTS

PROTEIN is essential for building and maintaining the muscles and tissues in your body and can also help control your appetite. By ingesting protein, you will feel fuller for longer. Optimum daily protein intake should be 25-35% of your daily calorie intake, but it depends on age, body size, and gender.
One gram of protein = four calories

CARBOHYDRATES are the body's primary energy source for your body and brain, including simple sugars and starchier complex carbohydrates. Your body can use carbohydrates immediately or store them as glycogen (sugar) in tissues. Complex carbohydrates can also be converted to fat. Between 40-55% of daily caloric intake should come from complex carbohydrates.
One gram of cho = four calories

FAT provides the highest concentration of energy for the body. 1lb of stored fat provides approximately 3,500 calories of energy. Fat is the primary fuel source for endurance sports such as marathons and ultra-marathons. It is needed during high-intensity exercise, where carbohydrates are the main fuel source to help access the stored glycogen (sugar).

However, using fat fuel for activity depends on these important factors:
1. Because fat is slow to digest, it can take up to 6 hours to be converted into a usable form of energy.
2. The body needs to break down the fat and transport it to the working muscles before it can be used as energy.

3. Converting the fat into energy takes a lot of oxygen, so exercise intensity must decrease for this process to occur.

Even though overeating fat can cause heart disease, fats are essential for good health, and 20 - 30% of your daily calories should come from healthy fats. One gram of fat = nine calories

Additional notes:

_____

_____

_____

_____

_____

TESTIMONIAL:

I am so thankful to have participated in the bodyFIT program. The six weeks went by quickly, with lasting results for me.

I am more in control of my food intake by being more aware of the nutritional value of my food. I had good results by shedding a few pounds! I enjoyed the workout classes and can see positive changes in my body; it's stronger and leaner. I will continue with the program concepts in my life going forward. I'm so grateful.

Brenda S. | BC Canada

FOODS, THEIR CALORIES, AND HOW LONG IT TAKES TO BURN THEM OFF

FAVOURITE TREAT FOODS	CALORIES	WORK IT OFF (In minutes)		
		Walking	Running	Biking
Starbucks Cranberry Orange Muffin	410	106	44	58
Starbucks White Hot Chocolate w/o whip (16 oz)	480	124	51	68
Starbucks Latte with skim (16oz)	100	26	11	14
Bagel - 3 ½" with 2 tbsp low-fat cream cheese	361	92	38	51
French baguette, 2oz	150	39	16	21
Quaker Instant Apple cinnamon oatmeal	130	33	14	18
Homemade muffin (2oz)	169	44	18	24
Krispy Kreme donut	200	52	21	28
Apple pie, 1/8th piece	411	106	44	58
French Fries, medium	380	98	40	54
French Fries, small	250	64	27	35
Snickers, Butterfinger	280	72	30	40
M&M's, Reese's peanut butter cups, Kit Kat	230	59	24	33
Dove rich dark chocolate, two squares	84	22	9	12
Jr. mints, 16	170	44	18	24
Granola Bar, Nature Valley	90	23	9	13
Luna's chocolate pecan pie energy bar	180	46	19	26
Egg rolls, 1	320	83	34	46
Steak, broiled tenderloin, 3 oz	220	57	23	31
Peanuts, approx. 32	165	43	18	23
Buttered popcorn, 7 cups	590	152	63	84
Redenbacher's smart pop microwave popcorn, 2 cups	30	8	4	4
Skinny Cow low-fat ice cream sandwich	140	36	15	20
Medium pop	140-150	36	15	20
Bottled water	0			

HEALTHY EATING TIPS

1. Purchase more fresh vegetables, fruit, whole grains, rice, fresh meats, poultry, fish, eggs, milk, and yogurt. These foods are naturally low in sodium.

2. Reduce the amount of salt used to prepare foods.

3. Use commercially prepared foods as little as possible; less than five ingredients should be listed (if any). Foods generally high in salt include cheeses (mainly processed cheese), luncheon and deli meats, canned soups and vegetables, bullion, crackers, cookies, packaged casserole mixes, snack foods, frozen foods, and fast foods.

4. Limit seasonings and sauces high in sodium, such as ketchup, relish, bouillon cubes, broth, soya sauce, barbeque sauce, fish sauce, black bean sauce, etc.

GUIDELINES FOR HEALTHY RESTAURANT EATING AND DRINKING

Try not to eat out during the 8-week program unless it's your treat day or a special occasion.

- Check out menus online before choosing a restaurant. Look for healthy meal options.
- Ask for a glass of water upon seating; if available, get a jug brought to the table.
- Avoid restaurants that have an "All You Can Eat" option.
- Order salad dressings and sauces on the side and add only a tiny amount to your meal.
- Pass on the bread and rolls offered complimentary or with meals.
- Try to stick to tomato-based meals and sauces rather than cream-based ones.
- Choose one of the three B main dishes: boiled, broiled, or baked. Stay away from anything fried.
- Choose chicken or fish; avoid fatty meats like duck and goose.
- If it's an option, choose salad instead of fries. It's a great way to load up on your veggies. If the choice is unavailable, sub a baked potato for the fries.
- If you have dessert, order fresh fruit or sherbet; avoid pastries and whipped cream desserts.
- Drink your water before your meal. Eat slowly and listen to your body when it's full. Ask for a to-go box for your leftovers.

Always have healthy snacks in your purse or car whenever possible; it can ward off hunger pains.

FIBRE FACTS

Dietary fibre is part of plant foods that cannot be digested. As well as fibre keeping the bowel in good working order, dietary fibre may also help to prevent chronic diseases such as diabetes, cardiovascular disease, colon cancer, and diverticular disease.

TYPES OF DIETARY FIBRE

The components that make up dietary fibre are grouped into two major types: soluble and insoluble. Plant foods vary considerably in the amount and types of fibre they contain.

SOLUBLE FIBRE

Soluble fibre dissolves in water. Eating foods containing soluble fibre helps control blood sugar levels by slowing the body's absorption rate. Soluble fibre also helps lower blood cholesterol when included in a low-fat diet.

Good Sources of Soluble Fibre

- Oat bran

- Oatmeal, Psyllium and Barley

- Pectin-rich fruits: apples, citrus fruits, bananas, strawberries

- Some veggies: potatoes with skin, green peas, carrots, broccoli

INSOLUBLE FIBRE

Insoluble fibre may help prevent or treat some colon diseases and reduce the risk of colon/rectal cancers. Also known as "roughage," this type of fibre helps to keep you regular. Since insoluble fibre increases the bulk of food, it can make you feel fuller, which may cause you to eat less.

Good Sources of Insoluble Fibre

- Wheat Bran and wheat bran cereals

- Whole grain foods such as whole wheat or rye bread, brown rice

- Legumes: dried peas, beans, and lentils

- Fruits and vegetables: skins and seeds add even more fibre

- Nuts and nut butter

HOW MUCH FIBRE SHOULD I EAT?

Aim for 25-35 grams of total dietary fibre each day. You can quickly achieve this goal without using supplements by eating a healthy, well-balanced diet. Choose fibre-rich foods to get a healthy balance of soluble and insoluble fiber to obtain all the benefits of fibre.

WHAT ABOUT WATER?

Fibre absorbs water, so you must drink enough water as you ingest fibre. Without enough fluid, a high-fibre diet may cause constipation. As mentioned, aim for at least 8-10 cups of water daily.

FLUIDS & HYDRATION

Our body weight is approximately 60% water, our brain is 70% water, and our lungs are nearly 90%. Humans can go weeks without eating but only a few days without water; we need water to survive.

HOW IMPORTANT ARE FLUIDS?

Fluid replacement is the most important nutritional concern for everyone on the road to health and fitness.

As you exercise, fluid is lost through your skin as sweat and through your lungs when you breathe. If this fluid is not replaced regularly during exercise, you can become dehydrated.

When dehydrated, you have a smaller volume of blood circulating through your body. Consequently, the amount of blood your heart pumps with each beat decreases, and your exercising muscles do not receive enough oxygen from your blood.

Proper fluid replacement is the key to preventing dehydration and reducing the risk of heat injury during training/exercise.

PREVENTING DEHYDRATION

Dehydration is more common than you think and can disguise itself as hunger. If your lips are feeling dry, you are probably already dehydrated. Often people are unaware that they are losing body fluid or that their performance is impacted by dehydration. The best way to prevent dehydration is to maintain body fluid levels by drinking plenty of fluids before, during, and after your workout.

If you are unsure how much fluid to drink, you can monitor your hydration using one of these two methods:

1. Weight: Weigh yourself before exercising and again after exercising. For every pound you lose during the workout, you must drink 2 cups of fluid to rehydrate your body.
2. Urine color: Check the color of your urine. You are dehydrated if it is dark gold, like apple juice. If you are well hydrated, the color of your urine will look like pale lemonade.

Thirst is not an accurate indicator of how much fluid you have lost. You are already dehydrated if you wait until you are thirsty to replenish body fluids. Most people do not become thirsty until they have lost more than 2% of their body weight; if you only drink enough to quench your thirst, you may still be dehydrated.

Keep a water bottle available when working out, and drink as often as possible.

Our body uses water to help regulate temperature and to maintain bodily functions. Because we lose water through breathing, perspiration, urination, and digestion, it's important to rehydrate by drinking fluids and eating foods that contain water daily.

Water does more than quench your thirst and regulate your body's temperature. It also keeps the tissues in your body moist. Do you know how it feels when your eyes, nose, or mouth gets dry? Keeping your body hydrated helps it retain optimum moisture levels in these sensitive areas and the blood, bones, and brain. Water helps protect the spinal cord and acts as a lubricant and cushion for your joints.

Each day, your body must replace approximately 2.5 liters of water through ingested liquid and foods.

Many mineral nutrients are also essential for maintaining fluid balance in the body. A few that come to mind are potassium, calcium, phosphorus, and magnesium. You can easily find information on these four minerals online or at your local Nutritionist's office.

The most familiar one is plain old table salt - Sodium. Sodium helps your body absorb and retain more water. To function normally, most adults require approximately 500mg of sodium daily, and athletes need up to 2000mg of sodium. Unfortunately, most people get too much sodium, usually from their diet. Too much salt retains excess fluid, making you feel bloated and affecting your heart function and blood pressure.

HOW MUCH WATER SHOULD YOU DRINK A DAY?

Most health authorities say we should drink at least eight cups (2 litres) of water daily. Others say that water needs vary by individual, and you should let thirst guide your intake. But your individual water needs depend on many factors, including your health, activity, and where you live. No single formula fits everyone.

Many people ask, "Can you drink too much water?" I've read that healthy people can't drink themselves to death on water. There are some illnesses, though, that water intake should be kept to a minimum while under the guidance of a health professional. These illnesses include cardiovascular disease, high blood pressure, and heart failure. Too much fluid in your body can make it harder for a weakened heart to pump.

How about not enough water? The body is 60% water, so we must drink a lot daily. Daily inconsistency in drinking water can cause the body to retain the fluid you have drank, making you feel bloated and gaining weight.

STILL NOT SURE IF DRINKING WATER IS FOR YOU? LOOK AT THESE BENEFITS:

- Increases energy and relieves fatigue
- Promotes weight loss
- Flushes out toxins
- Maintains regularity
- Boosts immune system
- Relieves headaches
- Prevents muscle cramping
- Improves your skin and complexion - water plumps your skin, leaving it clear, healthy, and resilient
- Prevents dehydration
- Supplies muscles with the enhanced ability to contract.

How can you make drinking water become a habit for you? I believe that drinking a consistent amount is essential and that you should drink the same amount of water EVERY DAY and have it with you. In the bodyFIT program, you will exercise intensely at least 3x a week and need to replace lost fluid, so I recommend at least 8 cups of water daily.

You will track your water intake daily, and when you first start drinking more than usual, you'll feel like you're always going to the bathroom, but it will only last a few days. Once you consistently drink the same amount of water daily, your body will hit a point of equilibrium, and you'll get into a regular rhythm of going to the bathroom every 2-3 hours instead of every hour. Please track how many glasses you drink daily by logging them in your nutrition logs.

So how do you get into the habit of drinking 8 cups of water a day? Here are a few examples:

- Upon waking, have 2 cups of warm water to awaken the body.
- Set your alarm for every hour, and then pour yourself a cup of water. At the hour when the alarm goes off, drink what is in the cup and fill it up again. Continue doing this every hour until you have consumed your 8 cups.
- Carry a 4-cup (1 litre) water bottle and fill it twice daily.
- Put four hair elastics around a 2-cup bottle. Every time you empty the bottle, take one of the elastics off.
- Let your bottle become your best friend. Carry it everywhere with you! Your body will thank you.

THINK BEFORE YOU DRINK

Is alcohol good for the heart? Don't start celebrating just yet. Before you reach for that beer or glass of wine, consider these questions:

Are you trying to manage your weight? Alcohol contains empty calories. Often alcohol is consumed in a social situation where food is also plentiful, which can mean more calories. Do you choose mixed drinks or cocktails? These are usually higher in calories.

Do you have high blood pressure? Too much alcohol may aggravate this problem.

Do you have high triglycerides? (the main constituents of natural fats and oils.) You may have to avoid alcohol or drink it occasionally if your level is elevated.

Do you have diabetes? Do you have reasonable blood sugar control? If not, you may want to avoid alcohol until your blood sugars are better controlled.

If you drink alcohol, do so in moderation. Moderation is considered two drinks/day for men and one drink/day for women. One drink is equal to:

- 12 oz beer
- 4 oz wine
- 1.5 oz spirits or liqueurs (Rye, Rum, Scotch, Vodka, Grand Marnier, etc.)

Remember, though, that you have purchased this program because you have a goal to achieve. Alcohol doesn't contain any nutritional calories at all. Save your favourite bevvie for your treat day (more to come about that.)

CALORIC VALUES OF ALCOHOL

Type of Alcohol	Serving Size	Calories
Regular Beer	12 oz	140-150
Lite/Light Beer	12 oz	100
Wine – White/Red	4 oz	80-90
Spirits: Rye, Rum, Vodka, etc.	1.5 oz	100
Mixed Drink	1.5 oz spirit+ 6 oz Juice/Pop	175
Cooler/Hard Lemonade	12 oz	200-300
Pina Colada	6 oz	350
Marguerita	6 oz	370

Additional notes:

_____

_____

_____

_____

_____

FOUR IMPORTANT "Q & As"

1: Does my fat turn into muscle?

A: Fat and muscles are two different compositions; it's like comparing apples and oranges. As you can see below, 5lbs fat is much bigger than 5lbs muscle. The reason? Muscle is much denser than fat, so it takes up less space in your body.

FACT: Lose 10 lbs of fat and gain 10 lbs of muscle, and you look and feel fantastic. But the scale shows "no progress!" What to do? TOSS THE SCALE!

2: How do I get rid of the fat? How does it leave my body?

A: Our body stores fat in fat cells in a form known as triglycerides. Triglycerides can't be used directly for energy, but when your body senses a calorie deficit, it breaks them down into glycerol and fatty acids that get released into the bloodstream. The glycerol and fatty acids are then used to create fuel for energy to support essential body functions, chores, and exercise. As a result, the fat cells shrink but never disappear.

Fat consists of three elements: carbon, hydrogen, and oxygen. When the triglycerides break down, it unlocks the carbon stored in the fat cells, creating carbon dioxide and water. The chemical reaction produces heat as a byproduct, but that isn't how the fat leaves your body. The fat excretes about 85 percent carbon dioxide through the lungs and 15 percent water through your urine, feces, sweat, and tears.

Exercise helps you lose fat more quickly because it increases your need for fuel and creates a more significant calorie deficit. When you consistently consume more calories than you use, your body returns to filling up the deflated fat cells, and you gain weight.

3: How is fat stored and burned as energy?

A: A small amount of fat is essential to a healthy diet. As well as providing the body with energy, fats regulate body temperature, reduce inflammation, help with blood clotting, and brain development. Excess fat is stored in the body's cells until it is needed for energy. When the body requires more energy, it will burn stored fat in a chemical process known as metabolism.

4: What is healthy blood pressure?

A: Blood pressure is measured by two numbers: The larger top number is systolic (the blood pressure when the heart is contracting), and the smaller bottom number is diastolic (the heart refills with blood after emptying.)

(mmHg stands for millimeters of mercury, and it measures pressure.)

- Healthy blood pressure is 120/80mmHg or lower
- High blood pressure is 140/90mmHg

Pressures such as 130/85 mmHg should be treated as a wake-up call to make some lifestyle changes since they, too, are associated with an increased risk of disease.

Keeping A Check On High Blood Pressure

High blood pressure, or hypertension, is a common medical problem and one of the critical risk factors for heart disease, stroke, and kidney disease. If you have been diagnosed with high blood pressure, the following tips may help you:

- Lose weight if needed. Even small weight losses can make a difference.
- Restrict your sodium intake to 1000/1500 mg or less per day. A diet high in salt (sodium) causes your body to hold on to (retain) fluid. This fluid build-up makes your heart work harder and can also build up in your lungs, making breathing harder. As mentioned earlier, it will also show weight gain.
- Avoid alcohol.
- Increase your potassium intake. (Make sure you check your potassium levels with your doctor). Foods that are rich in potassium lessen the effects of sodium. Eat some potassium-rich vegetables and fruit daily: cantaloupe, broccoli, oranges, bananas, carrots, prunes, spinach, and squash, to name a few. The more potassium you eat, the more sodium you lose through urine. Potassium also helps to ease tension in your blood vessel walls, which helps further lower blood pressure.
- Have 2 – 4 servings of milk products daily for calcium and eat fish rich in omega-3 fat twice a week.

TESTIMONIAL:

bodyFIT has changed my life. Before this program, I talked to my doctor about taking blood pressure medication; I am only 47 years old. After six weeks, my blood pressure returned to where I was in my 30s. No blood pressure medication for me!

This program brought to light how much sodium I was consuming daily. The awareness I have now and the changes I have made have helped me feel better and have more energy, and I want to continue with this way of life. I am so thankful for this program.

Amy R. | BC Canada

TESTIMONIAL:

Two weeks into the bodyFIT program, I felt more toned and stronger. Having the daily food/water journal and nutritional information helped.

I really enjoyed all the workouts too. I quickly got on track with my diet after realizing I wasn't eating enough. Thank you, coach!
Myrna H. | BC Canada

Additional notes:

_____
_____
_____
_____
_____
_____
_____
_____

Additional notes:

_____
_____
_____
_____
_____
_____
_____
_____
_____

Additional notes:

_____
_____
_____
_____
_____
_____
_____
_____
_____

METABOLISM

Metabolism is the rate at that you burn the calories you eat and drink.

Any movement you do speeds up your metabolism, including fidgeting! Increasing body temperature increases your metabolism by 14%, and eating protein does the same!

When you sleep, your metabolic rate decreases by 10%, and when you fast for more than 12 hours, your metabolic rate reduces by 40%.

WAYS TO BOOST YOUR METABOLISM NATURALLY

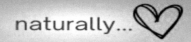

Ways to boost your metabolism

1. Drink plenty of water
2. Get 7-8 hours of sleep nightly
3. Drink green tea
4. Eat small meals often
5. Have some form protein with each meal
6. Choose some high-fibre foods for your meals
7. Perform high intensity exercise programs
8. Incorporate strength training into your workouts
9. Incorporate cardio into your workouts
10. Make sure to stretch after your workouts
11. Laugh and smile often

naturally...♡

THE bodyFIT PROGRAM

Six weeks of:

One full body workout - 3x week, every other day consisting of a combination of:

- HIIT training
- Core exercises
- Wait training (aka stretching)

to

- Strengthen the body
- Burn fat
- Improve mobility, balance, and flexibility.

Cardio 2-3x week (20-30 minutes at medium intensity).

SIX WEEKS TO A BRAND-NEW LIFE

Over the next six weeks, this could be your transformation:

- Lose 5-10 inches in overall body size
- Increase your strength, flexibility, posture, balance, and mobility
- Be more aware of the foods you eat; knowledge is power
- Make better choices in all areas of your life
- Begin living the life you want!

These are just a few possibilities you can create by committing to bodyFIT. You deserve to live an extraordinary life!

STRENGTH TRAINING AND CARDIO

Strength training burns calories and stimulates our muscles to grow stronger and leaner, protects bone health, and boosts metabolism. Cardio training strengthens our heart, lungs, and immune system and helps us achieve our fitness goals.

HIIT (High-Intensity Interval Training) is the secret ingredient in bodyFIT. Combined with what you'll be eating, this fun fitness program blending strength training and cardio is what you will be doing at least 3x a week.

HIIT is an interval training workout that takes you to your maximum target heart rate in a very short period of time. It combines several rounds of high-intensity movements followed by short periods of lower-intensity movements and keeps the body guessing throughout your workout. Each workout is tailored to your fitness level to make you feel successful at the end of the class.

After each HIIT workout, your body must recover and restore its resting state (homeostasis). This recovery is where the magic happens!

E.P.O.C. (Exercise Post Oxygen Consumption) is the amount of oxygen required to restore your body to homeostasis (rest) after exercise. Basically, our body puts out more calories during our recovery after exercise than before we exercise.

Your body will continue to burn more calories after you finish your workout, up to 24 hours! Your body will need at least 48 hours between workouts to help repair your muscles and aid recovery, and this is why it is vital to space your HIIT workouts every other day.

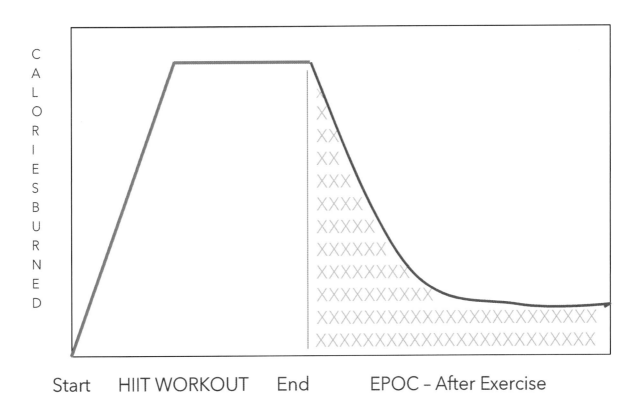

Start   HIIT WORKOUT   End   EPOC – After Exercise

NUTRITION

Have you heard the phrase "You are what you eat"? Nutrition is the study of the nutrients in food at work in our bodies, one energy source that keeps us alive. Proper nutrition is about eating a healthy and balanced diet; food and drink provide the energy and nutrients you need to be healthy. Understanding what you eat and drink is important because what you ingest daily dramatically impacts how your body functions and feels.

Though I am not a Nutritionist, I have read a lot of research over the past 30 years that I have put to use in my life, and I know that it's vital to understand what you are putting in your mouth if you want to make considerable changes in the way you look and feel about yourself. Knowledge is power, and when you understand what eating the right and wrong foods can do for your body, you will continue making the right food choices to live a healthy lifestyle.

I believe that food is one of life's pleasures, but we must be smart about what we eat and drink. Every day, we need to balance our food intake with some form of exercise to burn off those extra calories we consume. Food and drink provide the energy and nutrients you need to be healthy. Understanding what you eat and drink is important because what you ingest daily dramatically impacts how your body functions and feels.

Believe in the 80:20 rule. This rule concerns eating healthy. You will eat well-balanced meals for six days, combining protein, complex carbohydrates, and fats, and one day a week (it has to be the same day every week); you get to have a TREAT day. This day you get to indulge in your favourite foods.

Nutrition and exercise; the two go hand in hand. The calories you ingest should always equal or be less than the calories you burn. bodyFIT is not a diet. Combining balanced meals and incorporating exercise 3-5x a week are two of the best ways to become the best version of yourself. By eating enough of the right foods and combining them with strength training and cardio, you will learn how your body will become stronger, leaner, and burn fat efficiently.

I believe education is essential, especially when putting food into our bodies. "You are what you eat" rings true; many people have no idea what is in their food - the fat content and the amount of sodium and sugar.

Food portions: Use the chart below to help you gauge the most appropriate amount for each food type.

FOOD	PORTION SIZE
Rice or Gluten-Free Pasta	Size of a lightbulb (1/2 cup)
Baked potato (5 oz)	Size of a computer mouse
Whole grain/wheat Bagel (half)	Size of a hockey puck
Whole grain/wheat Muffin	Size of a large egg
Meats	Size of your palm
Nuts	Size of a ping pong ball
Butter	Size of the tip of your thumb
Cheese	Size of two dice
Raw vegetables	Size of your fist (1 cup)
Cooked vegetables	Size of a lightbulb
Fruit	Size of a tennis ball

SUCCESS WITH YOUR FOOD AND DRINK CHOICES

1. You must be mindful of two things in your meal planning for the next six weeks: your sodium and sugar intake:
   1) Sodium, try to keep your sodium intake to 1500-1700 mg daily
   2) Sugar, you should limit it to 5 mg or under per meal.

2. Read food labels when grocery shopping. This one can be a life changer for you. It will increase your awareness of calories, carbs, fats, proteins, sodium, and sugar.

3. Try to choose only from the foods shown on page 21 and eat various foods. For snacks, eat as many veggies as you want.

4. On your treat day, include some of the foods shown in the chart on page 55. Variety is the spice of life, and I believe that balance is needed when choosing our food.

5. Do not skip meals. If you are not home, carry snacks and meals with you.

6. Water - Consistency is key. Remember, throughout the day, try to drink 6-8 cups of water; herbal teas also count. Whichever amount you choose, be consistent, and your body will thank you. Don't forget to take your water bottle with you, and let it be your best friend!

7. Avoid cakes, pastries, cookies, ice cream, and anything else made with white flour and sugar.

HEART RATES

To ensure you are getting the most from your workouts, yet staying at a safe level, you can monitor how hard your heart is working. Aiming for a "target heart rate" can help you do this. Think of it as the "sweet spot" between not exercising hard enough and overexerting.

Resting heart rate: The rate at which your heart beats at rest. The more fit you are, the lower your resting heart rate. The average resting heart rate is between 60 and 100.

After resting/sitting for a few minutes, find your pulse. (Follow the bone of your thumb down just below the wrist, and gently move your fingers to the gap below the bone). Count the number of beats in a minute—your resting heart rate. (Alternately, you can take your pulse for 30 seconds and double it.)

	RESTING HR (RHR.) FOR WOMEN					
AGE	EXCELLENT	GOOD	ABOVE AVERAGE	AVERAGE	BELOW AVERAGE	POOR
18-35	61-64	65-68	69-72	73-76	77-82	83+
36-55	60-65	66-69	70-73	74-77	78-83	84+
56 +	60-64	65-68	69-72	73-76	77-84	85+

	RESTING HR (RHR) FOR MEN					
AGE	EXCELLENT	GOOD	ABOVE AVERAGE	AVERAGE	BELOW AVERAGE	POOR
18-35	56-61	62-65	66-70	71-74	75-81	82+
36-55	57-63	64-67	68-71	72-76	77-83	84+
56+	57-61	62-65	66-69	70-73	74-81	82+

<u>Maximum heart rate (MHR)</u>. The speed at which your heart can beat without causing any injury to it. The number is based on your age and subtracted from 220.

<u>Target heart rate (THR)</u>. The range of numbers reflects how fast your heart should beat when you exercise. This number is generally expressed as a percentage (usually between 50 and 85 percent) of your maximum safe heart rate. During exercise, you monitor your heart rate and try to reach the target zone.

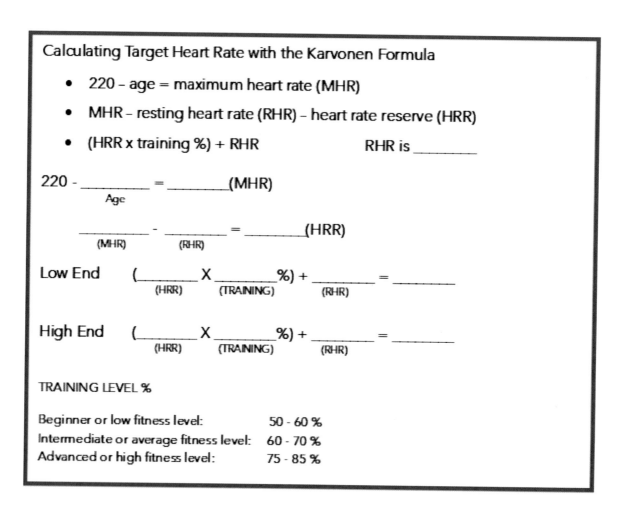

*The Korvonen formula was created by a Scandinavian physiologist, Martti Karvonen (1918-2008)

RATE OF PERCEIVED EXERTION

The Borg Rate of Perceived Exertion Scale (RPE) is a way to measure the level of exertion a person feels during physical activity. It is a valuable tool that helps people manage the intensity of their physical exercise.

The scale ranges from 6 to 20, allowing people to determine their level of exertion by how fast their heart is beating, how hard they are breathing, and more.

The Borg scale was the creation by Swedish scientist Gunnar Borg in the 1960s. He was interested in defining how a person perceived or felt exertion related to their body's physical response. Perceived exertion derives from the physical markers an individual may experience. These include:

- increased heart rate
- increased breathing rate
- increased sweating
- muscle fatigue.

When using the scale, a person must consider how they feel as a whole rather than focusing on one particular marker.

The table on the following page summarizes the ratings from the RPE scale.

When exercising, a person should aim for a rating between 12 and 16, which refers to the "moderate activity" level. If an individual is rating at 17 or higher, they can't stay here for long before they need to reduce the intensity of their workout to avoid potential injury or overexertion.

Rating	HOW THE EXERTION FEELS
6	**NO EXERTION** Doing nothing or resting
7.5	**EXTREMELY LIGHT EXERTION** Slightly increased heart rate. You should be able to talk while walking
9	**VERY LIGHT EXERTION** A gentle walk
11	**LIGHT EXERTION** A person has more than enough energy to continue exercising
13	**SLIGHTLY HARD EXERTION** Exercising is getting more difficult but is still manageable
15	**HARD EXERTION** Continuing the activity is noticeably more difficult
17	**VERY HARD EXERTION** A person can maintain this level of physical activity if they push themselves - they are very tired
20	**MAXIMAL EXERTION** Complete exhaustion

CARDIO BLAST WORKOUT

This cardio program is a quick, fast way to get your workout in quickly while walking, biking, or running. Rather than checking your heart rate, use the Borg RPE scale on the previous page to keep track of your progress.

	BEGINNER/BASIC OPTION	ADVANCED OPTION
Warm-up	6 min. at RPE 9-11	5 min. at RPE 9-11
Interval 1	2 min. at RPE 13 2 min. at RPE 14 2 min. at RPE 15 2 min. at RPE 16	3 min. at RPE 13 3 min. at RPE 14 2 min. at RPE 15 2 min. at RPE 16
Push #1	1 min. at RPE 17	1 min. at RPE 17
Recovery 1	5 min. at RPE 9-11	4 min. at RPE 9-11
Interval 2	2 min. at RPE 13 2 min. at RPE 14 2 min. at RPE 15 1 min. at RPE 16	3 min. at RPE 13 3 min. at RPE 14 2 min. at RPE 15 1 min. at RPE 16
Push #2	30 sec. at RPE 17	1 min. at RPE 17
Recover 2	5 min. at RPE 7.5	5 min. at RPE 7.5
Total Time	32.5 minutes	35 minutes

CARDIO JOURNAL

Use this sheet to keep track of your cardio. You can measure your work by the Target Heart Rates or the Borg RPE scale on pages 57-60. Try to get in at least 20-30 minutes a day, twice a week, of some form of cardio - fast walking, treadmill, elliptical, bicycle, skiing, etc.

DATE	MACHINE	RPE	TIME	DISTANCE	M.P.H.	LEVEL

POWER UP YOUR POSTURE

Our body's strength begins from within. We must be strong through our centre so the body can move with stability, strength, grace, and ease. A strong core promotes excellent posture, balance on the inside, a boost of self-esteem, and confidence on the outside. The beauty of this exercise is that it can be performed any time of the day, anywhere. Try it.

Standing tall and breathing normally, bring your feet hip-width apart and your toes pointing forward.

Roll to the outsides of your feet and then roll from the balls of your little toes to your big toes. Feel the weight under the balls of your feet and the outer points of your heels.

- Lift the arches of your feet by tightening up the sides of your legs.
- Tighten the front of your thighs, lift your kneecaps (do not hyperextend your knees.), and let that energy float down the back of the legs. Your feet should feel very grounded.
- Think of your pelvis as a bowl of water. Tip water out the back, then move it forward as if tipping it out the front. Now move it to a position where you are not spilling water to the front or back.
- Pull your belly button in and up towards your rib cage without rounding your spine.
- Lift the ribs (with your hands) and, imagining it to be a box, sit it over the pelvis bowl. Place thumbs on the rib cage and middle fingers on your hip bones – they should be vertical to one another.
- Slide your shoulder blades down your back and bring them forward, latching them into place around the armpits.
- Lengthen the back of your neck, tipping the chin downward.
- Imagine your head is a balloon, and let it 'float' on top of your neck. Feel your spine lengthen even more.

You should feel stronger and taller immediately. Practice this at least three times a day, and in no time, this will become your natural posture. The next time you go for a drive in your car, sit up very tall in your seat and adjust your rear-view mirror. Constantly adjust your posture. When you begin to slouch, you won't be able to see out of your mirror. Don't adjust your rearview mirror again.

LET'S GET STARTED!

YOU'VE GOT THIS!

WORKSHEETS & ASSESSMENTS

GOAL SETTING

My 6-week goal is:

_____

My target date is:

_____

To reach my goal, I will do these three things:

    1. _____

    2. _____

    3. _____

I will know I have reached my goal because:

_____

Two things that will help me stick to reaching my goal are:

    1. _____

    2. _____

_____   _____

Signature   Witness

Date:_____

COMMITMENT CONTRACT

Begin your transformation today by following these simple steps...

- Grocery shop at least 1x week to stock up on fresh veggies, fruit, and other healthy choices.
- Keep track of your daily meals to keep your eating choices in check.
- Include protein with every meal. Balance your meals with protein, carbohydrates, and fat.
- Try to drink AT LEAST 8 cups of water a day. Be consistent.
- Eat three meals and one or two snacks daily, and avoid eating 3 hours before bedtime.
- Control your portion size. Use a smaller plate or bowl for eating.
- Eliminate any unhealthy temptations at work or home.
- Take part in the HIIT class 3x per week to elevate your workouts.
- Perform cardio exercises 2-3x per week.
- Take measurements at the beginning, the 3-week, and the 6-week mark.
- Control and manage your stress levels. Check out the wellness portion of the program to help you identify your stresses and how you can overcome them.
- Get at least 7-8 hours of sleep per night. Our body repairs and recovers when we sleep.
- Daily, move your body as much as possible. Take the stairs instead of the elevator, park your car away from the stores so you must walk, walk to pick up your mail, etc.

I commit to these steps for the duration of the bodyFIT program.

_____   _____
Participant's Signature   Witness

_____   _____
Date   Date

PARTICIPATION CONTRACT

I, _____, agree to follow the guidelines below for the entire 6-week program:

1. Participate in a minimum of 1 fitness training class at least 3x a week for six weeks.
2. Record all my meals so that I can keep track of my progress.
3. Write out my Gratitude Journal every morning or night.

_____   _____
Participant's Signature   Date

_____   _____
Witness   Date

To create success over the next six weeks, you need to believe that you can do this and will succeed in obtaining your goal.

For free videos on how to measure your body and complete the fitness assessments, go to:

www.rhonaparsons.com/bfmp

pw: Imexcited

BODY MEASUREMENTS

Date: _____   Age: ___   Height: _____

	Beginning Date:	Mid Assessment	Final assessment	Difference (1st assessment - final assessment)
Blood Pressure				
Resting H.R.				
Weight				
Measurements				
Chest				
Waist				
Hips				
Right Arm				
Left Arm				
Right Thigh				
Right Calf				
Left Thigh				
Left Calf				
Total inches				

INITIAL FUNCTIONAL FITNESS ASSESSMENTS

Date:_____

POSTURE					
Dominant Hand	Right	Left			
Head	Neutral	Forward	Flat	Tilted R L	Rotated R L
Upper Back	Neutral	Kyphotic	Flat		
Shoulder	Neutral	Dropped R L	Elevated R L	Forward	Winged Scapula
Pelvis -	Neutral	Lordosis Posterior Tilt	Hips level	Drop R L	Elevated R L
Q Angle	Normal	Excessive			
Patella	Normal	Medial Rotation R L	Lateral Rotation R L		
Feet	Normal	External Rotation R L	Internal Rotation R L	Weight Dist. L	R
Arch	Normal	Pronated-Roll in	Supinated-Roll out		

Additional Notes:

MOVEMENT ANALYSIS: Looking For Proper Joint Alignment/Form Without Pain		
Human X	L – QL Lat	R – QL Lat
Walking	Any twisting through the waist? Head Forward? Arm movement? Narrow Gait?	

SQUATS:

Feet hip to shoulder-width apart, chest lifted, abs engaged, arms reaching forward.

Slowly lower into the squat position, knees no lower than 90 degrees, then return to standing; pause. Repeat 7x

**Look for internal/external hip rotation, leaning to one side or the other, knees sliding forward beyond toes, heels lifting, and knees in line with feet.

LUNGES:

Feet are hip to shoulder-width apart, R foot fwd., L foot back with heel lifted.

Slowly lower your back knee towards the floor; return to standing. Repeat 5x for each leg.

**Look for hip, knee, and ankle alignment, Internal/External rotation of the hip, front knee sliding forward beyond toes, front heel lifting, and/or balance issues. Is there a difference on either side?

PULL: (Use tubing, Theraband, or cable pulley)

Stand. With feet hip to shoulder-width apart, chest lifted, abs engaged, knees slightly bent.

Perform a row by pulling elbows towards the back. Return to the start position.

**Observe whether you can keep your shoulders down and have the ability to move the shoulder blades back towards each other.

PUSH:

Perform a knee pushup. Hands should be outside of shoulder-width apart.

Lower to 90 degrees at the elbow and back up to starting position. Repeat 5-10x.

**Look for back swaying, shoulder stability/winging, poke neck (head dropping), and symmetry through both movement phases.

CORE:

Lie on your back with your knees bent and feet flat on the floor. Place a folded washcloth under the lower back and tip your pelvis towards the floor using your abs.

1. Maintain your lower back on the cloth and with your abs contracted; bring one leg up to 90 degrees at the knee and hip, then lower without arching the spine. Repeat with the opposite leg. No problem?   Move to #2

2. Lift one leg to 90 degrees; hold and bring the other leg up to 90 degrees without arching through the spine or *pooching the belly. No problem? Move to #3

3. Lower your heels to the floor while maintaining 90 degrees at the knees. Ideally, you should be able to keep pressure on your hand until your feet touch the base.

* A pooching belly is when your abdominal muscles pop (pooch) up during an exercise.

FLEXIBILITY - R.O.M. = Range of Motion
Record "G" good" or "N.I." – needs improvement

BUTTOCKS

Sit upright on a bench and place an ankle on the opposite knee.

Shin is somewhat parallel to the floor, good R.O.M.
Knee pointing slightly upward, limited R.O.M.

Is there a difference b/w the right and left sides?

Right_____ Left_____

HAMSTRINGS

Lie on your back with straight legs and a folded washcloth under your lower back. (There will be a gap between your lower back and the floor.)

Contract abs, flex the foot (toes to ceiling), and lift one straight leg as high as possible, not allowing your pelvis to tip onto the washcloth.

**How high can the leg be lifted before the knee bends or the spine presses into the floor? Ideally, 80 degrees, good R.O.M.

Right_____ Left_____

HIP FLEXORS

Lie on your back with straight legs and a folded washcloth under your lower back. Bring one knee to your chest.

**If hip flexors are tight, the straight leg will bend at the knee, and/or your head will lift off the floor, and your pelvis will tip towards the floor. Any difference on both sides of the body?

Right_____ Left_____

CHEST/BACK

Lie on your back, lower back off the floor, abs tight, and arms at your sides.

Slowly raise your arms and extend them overhead until they're resting on or towards the floor beside your head. Can you touch your hands, wrists, and elbows to the floor without arching the spine?

Right_____ Left_____

ROTATOR CUFFS

Lie on your back, lower back off the floor, abs tight, elbows directly out to the side of shoulders, hands pointing upward (goalpost arms).

Keeping elbows in position, rotate your forearms towards the floor beside your head.

Can you touch your hands and wrists to the floor without arching your spine?

Right_____Left_____

FRONT OF THIGHS

Lie on your front with your head resting on your hands and legs straight.

Bring one foot towards the glute. Do your hips lift off the floor?

Can you bend more than 90 degrees at the knee? Repeat with the other leg.

Right_____Left_____

BEFORE & AFTER PHOTOS

DATE: _____

DATE: _____

THE TOP 6 TIPS FOR SUCCESS

You must commit to these six crucial steps to jump-start your transformation:

TIP #1:

Eat healthily. Go through your pantry and cupboards and eliminate junk food. Remember, you are what you eat!

TIP #2:

Include protein in every meal in your daily meal plan.

TIP #3:

Take HIIT classes three days per week. Show up for every workout.

TIP #4:

Keep your water bottle with you at all times.

TIP #5:

Get at least 7-8 hours of sleep daily.

TIP #6:

Make consistent, intentional efforts. Believe in yourself. Set your goals, plan every day, and go for it. Visualize yourself already having achieved your goal!

MEAL JOURNALLING

Research shows that keeping track of what you eat is the number #1 way of controlling and reducing your caloric intake. The 6-week program recommends keeping track of your food and water intake, and every 7th day allows you to journalize and break down each meal which will help you stay on track.

How to keep track of your food intake:

1. Plan what you will eat in advance, either the evening before or the morning. Always have a great breakfast; it's fuel to start your day right.

 2. Keep your diary with you and write down what you've eaten immediately after. Used as a method of deciding what you will eat, this is a great way to plan your meals and keep you on track.

3. Drink your water! That bottle needs to become your best friend. Take it with you everywhere.

4. If you are an emotional eater, writing your feelings down before eating, you will begin to understand why you choose the foods you do. By seeing it in writing, you can get it under control when you realize that the reason you choose those comfort foods is not really about the food.

DON'T FORGET TO CHOOSE YOUR TREAT DAY!

For all the hard work and commitment you have made in the six days, you deserve to celebrate! Choose the same day every week to enjoy your favourite foods and drinks.

"Awareness is the beginning of change."

WELLNESS GUIDE

The seven principles of THE ART OF B.A.L.A.N.CE. will help you understand the importance of bringing that elusive balance into your life through fitness, health, and wellness.

BREATH = Mindfulness

AWARENESS = The beginning of change

LENGTHEN = Observation of self

ALIGNMENT = Actions

NEUTRAL = Balancing

CORE = Stress/anxiety

EXPERIENCE = Excitement = new experiences

BREATH
LET GO OF THE PAST; BE PRESENT

Being present is about simplifying life. It's about living in the moment and letting go of things out of our control. It's about not thinking of what has happened in the past or worrying about the future. The past as we know it is gone; we cannot bring it back or change it. The future is only an illusion, and when we continuously focus on tomorrow, we miss the moments right now.

So how do you get present? You take your focus to your breath. When we focus on our breathing, we give our mind something to do. We stop it from overthinking, from thinking about the past and stressing about the future.

AWARENESS
IS THE BEGINNING OF CHANGE

We are all here on this beautiful planet to experience love and peace; however, with everything going on in our world today, it is so easy to get caught up in all the fear and disharmony that so many people are experiencing.

Fear is a frustration of love and can show up as anger, frustration, anxiety, worry, terror, distress, and other feelings. So, we want to turn our attention to gratitude as this is the next step toward healing and bringing balance to our life. When we can truly love ourselves and be grateful for all we have, the fear we sometimes feel will dissipate, and we will begin experiencing inner peace.

Gratitude is an excellent tool to move the negative energy and make us feel good. We can say our gratitude aloud or write down our gratitude. Before sleeping at night or upon waking, think of three things you are grateful for. Be thankful for those things, feel them in your heart, and then write down WHY you are thankful.

Whatever works for you, choose the same time every day to acknowledge and express appreciation for where you are in your life and what you have, your home, career, car, family, etc. Write with heartfelt gratitude and feel the happy emotions bubble up to the surface.

A gratitude card is an excellent tool for writing down your desires. Do this every day and watch your life change! When you read out loud what you have written and believe you already have what you desire, you align yourself with your goals and desires through the Law of Attraction, the secondary Universal Law.

WONDERFUL THINGS HAPPENED TODAY!

I am grateful for

1. _____

_____

because _____

_____

2. _____

_____

because _____

_____

3. _____

_____

because _____

_____

LENGTHEN
LET GO OF SELF JUDGEMENT

It is so easy for us to judge ourselves, especially if we are working hard to make positive changes in our life. Those old habits that are still a part of us can creep in quickly, and before we know it, we've made a wrong choice.

Self-sabotage can kick in, and you fall back into bad habits. So, how can you stop making bad choices before they happen?

- Observe your thoughts
- Develop self-acceptance by letting go of judgements that don't serve you
- Practice positive self-talk by writing affirmations.

Affirmations are a great way to use words that invoke positive thoughts and change old thought patterns and choices. Here are some examples:

I am so happy and so grateful now that I
"Am making healthy food choices," "Am the creator of my world," "Love me!", "Let go of all the lies I tell myself."

Use the card below to write an affirmation that serves you best today. Make photocopies of it and place them all over your home and vehicle.

AFFIRMATION CARD

I am so happy and so grateful now that I:

_____

_____

_____

_____

_____

ALIGN
LET GO OF THINGS YOU CAN NOT CHANGE

"IT IS WHAT IT IS" is a truth-seeking statement. It is neither negative nor positive; it just IS. When something is out of your control, I think these words bring the situation to fruition.

Let go of things you have no control over. When you recognize "it is what it is" in any situation, you can immediately let go of all expectations and set yourself free, allowing yourself to move forward with courage and no judgement. When you realize that what is happening to other people, or what others think of you, is none of your business, life will become much lighter, and you will have the space and freedom to align yourself with all that truly matters to you.

Intentional living works by clarifying your WHY and aligning with what makes you feel alive. Being intentional allows you to live with freedom, joy, and in a state of growth.

What is your purpose in life? What gets you out of bed in the morning? Your life's purpose can guide your life decisions, influence your behaviour, and shape your goals. You may also want to use your life's purpose, helping and teaching others.

Do you have a life purpose? Write it below.

_____

_____

_____

NEUTRAL
SURROUND YOURSELF WITH POSITIVE PEOPLE

Human beings have always been significantly influenced by the people they hang out with, and sometimes that's not the best thing for us, especially if we are trying to create better life habits for ourselves.

Your 'tribe' should always support your choices and only have your best interest at heart. People who are constantly trying to sabotage your best intentions have no place in your circle.

"You are the average of the five people you spend the most time with." Jim Rohn

Be aware of who your circle is. Are there people in your life whose cup is always half empty? When you share ideas with them, they are never excited for you, and sometimes you wonder why they are in your life. If you are at this point, you need to take the time to come from a place of neutrality where you can weigh out both the positive and negative information on the person and decide which road you will take with them.

We outgrow people. I believe people come into our lives for a reason, season, or lifetime; some stay for a short time and then leave as fast as they arrive. It's okay to let them go. If you have people in your life who don't make you feel great when you are in their company, add their name to the table below and figure out whether you should work on the relationship or say goodbye.

CORE
LIVE AUTHENTICALLY

Some of us go through the facade of life wearing a mask and being who others expect us to be. We fill up our days serving others and taking on another's opinions, and we get caught up in this crazy world where we lose sight of who we are.

How can you live a happy, fulfilled life when you are not doing what you want to do? Living your life to please others is not living authentically! You can only live up to others' expectations for so long; eventually, the mold formed around you will crack and break.

Are specific thoughts/beliefs/feelings holding you back from being authentic?

_____

What thoughts/beliefs/feelings stop you from living your desired life?

_____

What do you want in life?

_____

EXPERIENCE
LIVE YOUR LIFE TO THE FULLEST

Take care of yourself, be happy, love deeply, and enjoy life to the fullest! Experience each day as if it is your last. Here's wishing you a beautiful day.

Be the loveable person you are. - Everyone else is already taken.

DAILY PRACTICE

When combining fitness, health, & wellness into your life, you will ultimately begin to bring balance to your body, mind, and spirit and start living the life you want. This section of the bodyFIT program will explore how to bring wellness to your daily life.

Again, as explained on page 23, upon waking every morning, try to create 30 minutes for yourself to help you set your day up for success.

Even if you must break up the 30 minutes into three 10-minute sections, it'll help you with your upcoming goals.

Don't go on your phone. When we go on our phones and check our emails, we are already dealing with someone else's business. The start of the day should begin with your business.

Water: Begin with drinking two cups of warm water. Warming the water is to have it at your body's temperature so it is readily digestible. Your body has fasted the entire night, and the water will awaken your internal organs.

Breathwork: After drinking warm water and making your favourite tea/coffee, find a quiet place to sit, and if you can/want to, find a lovely piece of relaxing music to play. Begin to focus on your breath, inhaling and exhaling, and stay with your breath for 5-10 minutes, allowing the body to wake up and begin your day with ease and grace.

Gratitude: *"Gratitude is the rich soil to start growing amazing things!"*

Don't forget to write out your gratitude card!

I AM HAPPY AND GRATEFUL FOR: DATE: _____

1._____

because_____

2._____

because_____

3._____

because_____

You can also write gratitude for seeing your ideal future as it is happening right now. This is a great way to bring all you desire into your life. Continue to do this daily, and you will begin to see life a little differently.

Happiness:

Before you begin your day, close your eyes, and ask: "How do I want to show up in the world today?". Notice the first word that comes to mind and take this word with you. Smile at everyone you meet. It'll make you feel good; you never know whose life you will change with just your smile. Go and have a wonderful day.

TESTIMONIAL:

I wholeheartedly recommend Rhona Parsons' Beyond The Scale program. It encompasses excellent components of physical exercise, nutrition, and a very beneficial mental aspect. The discussions around correctly refocusing our minds and measuring our "wellness" added a deeper layer to the fitness program.

My coach was so upbeat, supportive, and genuine that it made the classes a joy to attend and made you want to keep coming back. She was in tune with each individual and how their bodies were reacting, and she would take the time to advise how to adjust the exercises to that individual and additional steps they should take.

After six weeks, I gained noticeable strength and flexibility, went down 14 inches (and 8 lbs), and feel invigorated and encouraged to keep it up. I am looking forward to attending more classes! Thank you!

Dana S. | BC Canada

Additional notes:

_____

_____

_____

_____

_____

_____

_____

_____

ARE YOU READY?

Just remember:

The difference between

TRY

and

TRIUMPH

is a little

UMPH!

TAKE SMALL STEPS

EVERY DAY...

EQUIPMENT NEEDED

DUMBBELLS

Using dumbbells in our workouts is a great way to build strength, increase muscle mass (don't worry, ladies – you aren't going to get big), and create muscular endurance (the ability to perform a movement for some time without getting tired.) They also allow us the flexibility to modify exercises; any person of every fitness level can use them.

You will notice in the weekly workouts that each workout is different. Your body will be challenged by doing more or fewer sets per exercise per muscle group, and sometimes the repetitions of one exercise will change. This weight change and the number of repetitions you will be doing will keep your body thinking. By changing repetitions, timing, and different variations of exercises, the changes you are looking for in your body will happen.

Picking the right dumbbell weights depend on your exercise goals in the program. The two different options we want to achieve are:

Goals	Repetitions	Dumbbell Size(s)
To build strength and muscle mass	8 - 12	
To increase muscular endurance	12 - 18	

At the beginning of the program (especially if this is the first time you have used dumbbells), you should be able to do 12 repetitions with control and great form. When you can perform 14 repetitions with the same weight and doing the same exercise, it's a great sign that you are getting stronger – and it's time to use heavier weights. Use the chart above to record the weights you will be using.

INSTRUCTIONS FOR SUCCESS!

The following pages are broken down into weekly segments.

#1: Weekly Agenda. This page is where you will write down the following:

- ✓ Your weekly goal
- ✓ A timetable of what your week looks like. Make sure to include your workouts
- ✓ A weekly affirmation. This powerful sentence you will create will get you through any setbacks you may incur during the week. Examples are shown on page 24.

#2: The Workout. Performed 3x during the week with a day off in between:

- ✓ The warmup
- ✓ The HIIT workout
- ✓ Cooldown
- ✓ Cardio suggestions for the days between the HIIT workouts.

#3: Meal Journalling. These sheets are where you will record the following:

- ✓ Your daily meals
- ✓ Your water intake
- ✓ Your emotions (how you felt during the day)
- ✓ Your gratitude thoughts.

Need some extra help? Looking for a coach?

For more information on how I can help you, go to:
www.rhonaparsons.com/bf

WEEK ONE

My weekly goal is:

_____

To reach my goal, I will do these three things each day:

Sunday	Monday	Tuesday	Wednesday
Thursday	Friday	Saturday	

Weekly Affirmation:

_____

_____

_____

HIIT 1
PERFORM 3X ALTERNATE DAYS IN THE WEEK
WARMUP: TOTAL: 4 minutes

1. ALT. STEP SIDE 2 SIDE

Start with feet together, step out to the side, bring feet together, and step to the other side. Repeat.

2. ALT. HAMSTRING CURLS

Start with feet apart and alternating legs, bring foot up to buttocks, pulling elbows back and squeezing shoulder blades together.

Exercises 1-8

Move 20-seconds / March 10 seconds

3. ALT. KNEE LIFTS

Start with feet hip-width apart and, alternating legs, twist and bring knee up to meet the opposite elbow.

4. ALT. SIDE REACHES

Start with feet wide and alternating arms, reach the arm up and tap out the same-side foot.

5. ALT. SHUFFLE SIDE 2 SIDE

Start with feet hip-width apart and, shuffle side 2 side for 3 steps, stopping with a hop, and then go in the other direction.

-----> <-----

6. SKIPPING

Start with feet hip-width apart, grab an imaginary skipping rope, and skip! Low impact option: Toes can stay on the floor.

7. ALT. FRONT PUNCHES

Start with feet wide, hinge from the hips, and engage abs. Twisting from the waist, extend arms out in front.

8. ALT. HEEL DIGS

Start with feet hip-width apart, hinge from the hips, and alternate bringing heels forward. Reach with arms.

LET'S GET STARTED!

FULL BODY WORKOUT

Perform exercises 1-8 for 40 seconds/rest 20 seconds.

Repeat once more.
Total time: 22 minutes
Challenge: Repeat 2 more times

Equipment needed: Dumbbells

* CHOOSE A WEIGHT THAT CHALLENGES YOU AT 12 REPETITIONS

1. Sumo Squats

2. Standing Rows X2 (Left and Right)

3. Curtsy Squats with Shoulder Presses X2 (Left and Right)

4. Plie Squats

5. Biceps Curls

6. Lunge Twists X2 (Left and Right)

7. Triceps Kickbacks

8. Good Mornings

PERFORM EACH EXERCISE FOR 40 SECONDS - 20 SECONDS REST

1. Sumo Squats

Stand tall with feet shoulder-width apart, abs connected, spine long. Inhale, hinge from the hips, squat down, keeping spine and neck in neutral. Exhaling, tighten glutes and come to standing. Pause, repeat.

2. Standing Rows - Right and Left

Begin with a split-stance, hinge forward from your hips, abs connected, and spine long.

Inhale and squeeze right shoulder blade towards spine as you bring the elbow up, pause, **exhale** and release. Repeat for 40 seconds. Change sides and repeat exercise.

3. Curtsy Squats with Shoulder Presses - Right and Left

Begin as shown with feet hip-width apart, shoulders down, and abs connected.

Inhale and squat, bringing right foot behind left in a curtsy manner. Exhaling, come to standing, tapping right foot out to side, and extending arms above head. Pause, repeat for 40 seconds. Change sides and repeat exercise.

4. Plie Squats

Stand with a wide stance, knees in line with toes, abs connected, spine long.

Inhale and squat down, hinging at hips, keeping spine and neck in neutral, chest lifted, and shoulders back. Exhaling, tighten glutes and come to standing. Pause, repeat.

5. Biceps Curls

Stand with arms at sides, palms facing inwards, shoulders down, abs tight.

Exhale as you slowly bring the weights up and turn the palms towards your shoulders. Keep elbows at sides.

Inhale, return to starting position and repeat movement.

6. Stationary Lunge Twists - Right and Left

Stand in a lunge position with left foot back, both feet and hips facing forward, shoulders down, abs tight. Hold a dumbbell between your hands at chest height.

Exhale as you slowly lower back knee towards the floor, pause and then twist upper body to the right. Inhale, come back to starting position. Repeat for 40 seconds. Change sides and repeat exercise.

7. Triceps Kickbacks

Stand in a lunge position with left foot back, both feet and hips facing forward, abs tight. Bring your elbows up to your sides and roll shoulders back and down.

Exhale as you straighten both arms, keeping elbows still in space; pause. **Inhale**, return back to starting position. Repeat.

8. Good Mornings

Begin in posture, abs connected, spine long.

Inhale; hinge forward from hips, keeping spine in neutral. **Exhale**, tighten glutes and come to standing. Pause,

Perform exercises 1-8 once more.

WAIT TRAINING

Static stretching is an important way to end your activity. This form of stretching is a holding stretch. We want to put our body in a specific position that will work on releasing tightness and will lengthen our muscles. If your body is relaxing in the stretch, you can stay there as long as it feels good. Some holding stances, though, need the contraction of the opposing muscle(s) to support the lengthening muscles. Hold each stretch for 20-50 seconds, whatever feels best for you.

CHEST OPENER

Chest: Roll your shoulders back and take your hands behind your back; clasp your hands together.

Squeeze your shoulder blades together to create an opening across your chest.

HAMSTRING LENGTHENER x2

Back of thigh: Set up as shown, shoulders relaxed. As you push down the front heel, lift buttocks up towards ceiling.

Repeat on the other side.

SIDE LYING BOW POSE x2

Front of thigh, chest and shoulder: Set up as shown. Bend bottom leg for balance.

Bring your knee forward and grab your ankle, pant hem, shoe, sock, whatever you need to slowly pull leg back and line up knee with front of hip. Roll shoulder back to open chest.

Repeat on the other side.

Modification: Keep leg bent and tap foot to the floor behind you.

HIP OPENER x2

Hip and front of body: Step back with one foot, legs hip-width apart.

Engage core, lower into a lunge, tighten buttocks, and reach same-side arm up and back.

Repeat on the other side.

SIDE x2

Side body: Place your left foot behind the right, reach your left arm up and over as you push out your left hip.

Repeat on the other side.

BACK

Back: Place your hands slightly above bent knees. Tuck tail under as you round your back. Hold for 2 breaths. Release and repeat 3 more times.

SWEET SPOT x2

Between shoulder blades and lower back: Reach over with your left hand and grab the outside of your right foot.

Slowly begin to pull back with your body and point your foot away. As the stretch begins to subside, tip your head to look under arm.

Repeat on the other side.

WEEK 1 – DAY 1

Breakfast:

_____
_____
_____ Time:

Lunch:

_____
_____
_____ Time:

Snack:

_____
_____
_____ Time:

Dinner:

_____
_____
_____ Time:

Snack:

_____
_____
_____ Time:

Water: ▽ ▽ ▽ ▽ ▽
▽ ▽ ▽ ▽ ▽

Today I am feeling:

_____
_____

I am grateful for:

_____
_____
_____

DAY 2

Breakfast:

_____
_____
_____ Time:

Lunch:

_____
_____
_____ Time:

Snack:

_____
_____
_____ Time:

Dinner:

_____
_____
_____ Time:

Snack:

_____
_____
_____ Time:

Water: ▽ ▽ ▽ ▽ ▽
▽ ▽ ▽ ▽ ▽

Today I am feeling:

_____
_____

I am grateful for:

_____
_____
_____

DAY 3

Breakfast:

_____
_____
_____ Time:

Lunch:

_____
_____
_____ Time:

Snack:

_____
_____
_____ Time:

Dinner:

_____
_____
_____ Time:

Snack:

_____
_____
_____ Time:

Water: ▽ ▽ ▽ ▽ ▽
▽ ▽ ▽ ▽ ▽

Today I am feeling:

_____
_____

I am grateful for:

_____
_____
_____

DAY 4	DAY 5	DAY 6
Breakfast:	Breakfast:	Breakfast:
_____	_____	_____
_____	_____	_____
_____	_____	_____
_____ Time:	_____ Time:	_____ Time:
Lunch:	Lunch:	Lunch:
_____	_____	_____
_____	_____	_____
_____ Time:	_____ Time:	_____ Time:
Snack:	Snack:	Snack:
_____	_____	_____
_____	_____	_____
_____ Time:	_____ Time:	_____ Time:
Dinner:	Dinner:	Dinner:
_____	_____	_____
_____	_____	_____
_____ Time:	_____ Time:	_____ Time:
Snack:	Snack:	Snack:
_____	_____	_____
_____	_____	_____
_____ Time:	_____ Time:	_____ Time:
Water: ▽▽▽▽▽ ▽▽▽▽▽	Water: ▽▽▽▽▽ ▽▽▽▽▽	Water: ▽▽▽▽▽ ▽▽▽▽▽
Today I am feeling:	**Today I am feeling:**	**Today I am feeling:**
_____	_____	_____
I am grateful for:	**I am grateful for:**	**I am grateful for:**
_____	_____	_____
_____	_____	_____
_____	_____	_____

DAY 7 Total cups of water:	TOTAL CALORIES	FAT (g)	CHO (g)	PROTEIN (g)	Sodium (mg) < 2000 mg per day	Sugars (g) < 5g per day
BREAKFAST:						
LUNCH:						
SNACK:						
DINNER:						
SNACK:						
TOTALS:		x9	x4	x4		

Today I am feeling: _____

I am grateful for_____

WEEK TWO

My weekly goal is:

_____

To reach my goal, I will do these three things each day:

Sunday	Monday	Tuesday	Wednesday
Thursday	Friday	Saturday	

Daily Affirmation:

_____

_____

_____

HIIT 2

PERFORM 3X ALTERNATE DAYS IN THE WEEK

WARMUP: TOTAL: 4 minutes

1. ALT. STEP SIDE 2 SIDE

2. ALT. HEEL DIGS

> Exercises 1-8
>
> Move 20-seconds / March 10 seconds

3. ALT. KNEE LIFTS

4. ALT. HAMSTRING CURLS

5. ALT. SIDE REACHES   6. SKIPPING (Imaginary skipping rope)

7. ALT. FRONT PUNCHES

8. ALT. SHUFFLE SIDE 2 SIDE

----->   <-----

CARDIO STRENGTH

FULL BODY WORKOUT

Perform exercises in 2s, 40 seconds each exercise
Rest 20 seconds.
(1, 2) (3, 4) (5, 6) (7, 8) (9, 10) (11, 12) (13, 14)

Total time: Approx. 22 minutes
Equipment needed: Dumbbells

* CHOOSE A WEIGHT THAT CHALLENGES YOU AT 12 REPETITIONS

1. Plie Squats with Dumbbell Raises

2. Skipping

3. Standing Rows (Left)

4. Alternating Lateral Step Jumps

5. Standing Rows (Right)

6. Wide Marching

7. Pushups

8. Alternating Toe Taps

9. Alternating Front Punches

10. Shuffles Side 2 Side

11. Alternating Curtsy Squats

12. Hamstring Curls

13. Alternating Triceps Extensions

14. Standing Knee Lifts with Twist, Right and Left (20 seconds each)

1. Plie Squats with Dumbbell Raises – 40 seconds

Stand tall with legs turned out (knees in line with toes), abs connected, spine long.

Inhale and hinging at the hips, lower down, raising arms to the front; Exhale and rise to standing. Repeat.

2. Skipping – 40 seconds

Imagine holding on to a skipping rope and begin to turn it from movement beginning at the shoulders.

Options:
Low impact: Keep toes on floor
Power jumping: Add a jump with each 'turn' of rope.

20-SECOND REST

3. (Left) Standing Rows – 40 seconds

Begin with a split-stance, abs connected, spine long.

Inhale, squeeze left shoulder blade towards spine as you bring the elbow up, pause. **Exhale** and release. Repeat.

4. Alternating Lateral Step Jumps – 40 seconds

Jump side to side, tapping your foot as you land.

Challenge: Land on one foot without tapping down.

----->   <-----

20-SECOND REST

5. (Right) Standing Rows – 40 seconds

Begin with a split-stance, abs connected, spine long.

Inhale and squeeze right shoulder blade towards spine as you bring the elbow up, pause. **Exhale** and release. Repeat.

6. Wide Marching – 40 seconds

Keep legs wide as you march on the spot, lifting knees, and moving arms (running arms).

Challenge 1: sink deeper into the legs

Challenge 2: Hop side 2 side

20-SECOND REST

7. Pushups – 40 seconds

Begin as shown. Take hands wide (elbows should be over top of wrists at lowest point). Abs tight, shoulders down, and **neck in line with spine.**

Inhale and **bend** your elbows (the body and head will follow). ONLY GO AS LOW AS YOU CAN KEEP YOUR FORM.

Exhale, push back up and repeat.

8. Alternating Toe Taps – 40 seconds

Begin lying on the mat and place elbows under the shoulders and hands flat on mat. Push elbows outward to stabilize shoulders.

Engage your abs and lift knees off mat, straightening legs. Alternate tapping toes out to the side, **exhaling** each time.

Modification: Begin with knees down, straightening leg as you tap toes.

20-SECOND REST

9. Alternating Front Punches – 40 seconds

Begin in a plie squat, abs connected, shoulders down, and spine long.

Keeping pelvis still and **exhaling** with each punch, twist through waist 'punching' forward, straightening arms.

10. Shuffles Side 2 Side – 40 seconds

Begin in a squat position, hinging at hips, abs tight, shoulders down.

Quickly step 3x to the side, ending with leg lifted; repeat to the other side.

----->   <-----

20-SECOND REST

11. Alternating Curtsy Squats – 40 seconds

Begin standing with feet hip-width apart, shoulders down, and abs connected.

Inhale and squat, bringing right foot behind left in a curtsy manner, stay low. **Exhale** back to centre, and repeat, bringing left foot behind right in a curtsy manner. Repeat side 2 side.

12. Alternating Hamstring Curls – 40 seconds

Stand with feet wide, abs tight, shoulders down.

Shift weight to one side and kick foot up towards the glutes. Place foot back down on the floor and kick towards glutes with the other foot. Repeat side 2 side.

20-SECOND REST

3. Alternating Triceps Extensions – 40 seconds

Stand with feet hip-width apart. Bend knees deeply, elbows at sides, abs connected, spine long.

Inhale and, simultaneously, slowly extend one arm straight out in front and one back, palms facing in. **Exhale** and come back to start. Repeat, alternating front and back arms.

14. Standing Knee Lifts with Twist, Right and Left – 20 seconds on each side

Stand with feet wide, shoulders down. Bring weight over to left shoulder, shifting weight to left foot.

Exhale, engage core and twist to the right, simultaneously lifting right knee. **Inhale**, release. Repeat moves for 20 seconds and then repeat with right shoulder and left knee.

BALANCE CHALLENGE

Perform the sequence 4 times.

Repeat on the other side.

Stand tall with your feet hip-width apart, engage the core, and bring elbows to your sides with your hands in front of your chest.

1. Inhale and slowly lift your knee.

2. Exhale, slowly extend your arms upwards, and straighten your front leg.

3. Inhale, bend your elbows, bring your hands in front of your chest, and bend your knee.

4. Exhale, hinge from your hip, simultaneously pointing your hands down towards the floor and extending your leg behind you, keeping hips in neutral with both hip bones pointing downwards. (Allow your gaze to follow the movement of your body).

Bring your body back to the starting position.

Challenge: Hold a dumbbell between your hands.

WAIT TRAINING

Hold each stretch for 20-50 seconds

CHEST OPENER   **HAMSTRINGS x2**   **HIP OPENER x2**

SIDE x2   **BACK**

SIDE LYING BOW POSE x2   **SWEET SPOT x2**

Week 2 - DAY 1	**DAY 2**	**DAY 3**
Breakfast:	Breakfast:	Breakfast:
_____	_____	_____
_____	_____	_____
_____ Time:	_____ Time:	_____ Time:
Lunch:	Lunch:	Lunch:
_____	_____	_____
_____	_____	_____
_____ Time:	_____ Time:	_____ Time:
Snack:	Snack:	Snack:
_____	_____	_____
_____	_____	_____
_____ Time:	_____ Time:	_____ Time:
Dinner:	Dinner:	Dinner:
_____	_____	_____
_____	_____	_____
_____ Time:	_____ Time:	_____ Time:
Snack:	Snack:	Snack:
_____	_____	_____
_____	_____	_____
_____ Time:	_____ Time:	_____ Time:
Water: ▽▽▽▽ ▽▽▽▽	Water: ▽▽▽▽▽ ▽▽▽▽	Water: ▽▽▽▽▽ ▽▽▽▽
Today I am feeling:	**Today I am feeling:**	**Today I am feeling:**
_____	_____	_____
I am grateful for:	**I am grateful for:**	**I am grateful for:**
_____	_____	_____
_____	_____	_____
_____	_____	_____

DAY 4

Breakfast:

_____

_____

_____ Time:

Lunch:

_____

_____

_____ Time:

Snack:

_____

_____

_____ Time:

Dinner:

_____

_____

_____ Time:

Snack:

_____

_____

_____ Time:

Water: ⏄ ⏄ ⏄ ⏄ ⏄
       ⏄ ⏄ ⏄ ⏄ ⏄

Today I am feeling:

_____

_____

I am grateful for:

_____

_____

_____

_____

DAY 5

Breakfast:

_____

_____

_____ Time:

Lunch:

_____

_____

_____ Time:

Snack:

_____

_____

_____ Time:

Dinner:

_____

_____

_____ Time:

Snack:

_____

_____

_____ Time:

Water: ⏄ ⏄ ⏄ ⏄ ⏄
       ⏄ ⏄ ⏄ ⏄ ⏄

Today I am feeling:

_____

_____

I am grateful for:

_____

_____

_____

_____

DAY 6

Breakfast:

_____

_____

_____ Time:

Lunch:

_____

_____

_____ Time:

Snack:

_____

_____

_____ Time:

Dinner:

_____

_____

_____ Time:

Snack:

_____

_____

_____ Time:

Water: ⏄ ⏄ ⏄ ⏄ ⏄
       ⏄ ⏄ ⏄ ⏄ ⏄

Today I am feeling:

_____

_____

I am grateful for:

_____

_____

_____

_____

DAY 7 Total cups of water:	TOTAL CALORIES	FAT (g)	CHO (g)	PROTEIN (g)	Sodium (mg) < 2000 mg per day	Sugars (g) < 5g per day
BREAKFAST:						
SNACK:						
LUNCH:						
SNACK:						
DINNER:						
TOTALS:		x9	x4	x4		

Today I am feeling: _____

I am grateful for_____

WEEK THREE

My weekly goal is:

_____

To reach my goal, I will do these three things each day:

Sunday	Monday	Tuesday	Wednesday
Thursday	Friday	Saturday	

Daily Affirmation:

_____

_____

_____

HIIT 3
PERFORM 3X ALTERNATE DAYS IN THE WEEK

WARMUP: TOTAL: 4 minutes

1. MARCHING IN/OUT

2. ALT. STEP TOUCH

Exercises 1-8

Move 20-seconds / March 10 seconds

3. ALT. KNEE LIFTS

4. ALT. SIDE REACHES

5. ALT. BOX TWISTS

6. ALT. REVERSE LUNGES

Start with feet hip-width apart and with alternating arms, alternate tapping one foot back.

7. ALT. SIDE BENDS

8. SKIPPING

Start with feet wide and hands behind your head, exhale and alternate bending to one side, meeting knee and elbow.

TONE n' TIGHTEN

FULL BODY WORKOUT

Perform exercises in 3s

1st exercise: work 40 seconds/rest 20 seconds.
2nd exercise: work 30 seconds/rest 15 seconds
3rd exercise: work 20 seconds/rest 10 seconds

Equipment needed: Dumbbells

* CHOOSE A WEIGHT THAT CHALLENGES YOU AT 12 REPETITIONS

1. Push Ups/Chest Presses/Chest Flyes

2. Reverse Lunges/Knee Lifts/Hops (Left)

3. Reverse Lunges/Knee Lifts/Hops (Right)

4. Double Rows/Triceps Kickbacks/Rear Delt Raises

5. Russian Twists/Supine Obliques/Alternating Arm Reaches

6. Plie Squats/Plie Squats with DB Flyes/Plie Jumps

7. Forearm Plank Holds/Toe Taps/Double Knee Drops

1. Pushups - 40 seconds' work/20 seconds' rest

Begin on the floor (as shown.) Place hands out wide with elbows lifted (but slightly behind shoulders), shoulders down, and abs really tight.

Exhale and push yourself up, keeping your torso connected (ribs and hips). **Inhale** and lower down. Repeat.

2. Chest Presses - 30 seconds' work/15 seconds' rest

Begin with feet hip-width apart, shoulders down, neck lengthened, and arms raised above shoulders with your palms facing forward, and weights touching. Engage core.

Inhale, at a quick pace (not losing form) lower your elbows to the floor, aligning up your wrists over your elbows. **Exhale,** using chest, press the weights back up, bringing them together. Repeat

Modification: Place a pillow under your head if your gaze is looking behind you.

3. Chest Flyes - 20 seconds' work/10 seconds' rest

Begin with feet hip-width apart, shoulders down, neck lengthened, and arms raised above shoulders with your palms facing inward, weights touching. Create a slight bend in your elbows. Engage core.

Inhale, at a quicker pace, lower your arms outwards, keeping the arms slightly bent, **Exhale,** using chest, bring weights back together. Repeat.

Modifications:

1. Place a pillow under your head if your gaze is looking behind you.
2. Only take arms out as far as you can maintain form.

Notes:

_____

_____

_____

_____

_____

_____

_____

_____

Perform the following three exercises with your left leg.

1. Reverse Lunges - 40 seconds' work/20 seconds' rest

Begin by hinging from hips, feet hip-width apart and right arm forward.

To master the move, **inhale,** tap left foot back and bring left arm forward. **Exhale,** bring foot forward with right arm. Repeat.

2. Reverse Lunge Taps/Knee Lifts- 30 seconds' work/15 seconds' rest

Begin with left foot back, hinging from hips, feet hip-width apart and left arm forward.

Exhale, tap foot forward and back faster (double time) lifting knee, making sure to change arms.

Modification: Stay with tapping foot to floor.

3. Reverse Lunge Knee Lifts/Hops - 20 seconds' work/10 seconds' rest

Begin with left foot back hinging from hips, feet hip-width apart and left arm forward.

Exhaling, bring leg forward and hop, lifting knee, making sure to change arms. Inhale, bring foot back to the starting position.

Modification: Lift knee rather than hop.

Repeat all three exercises with your right leg.

Notes:

_____

_____

_____

_____

_____

_____

_____

_____

1. Double Rows - 40 seconds' work/20 seconds' rest

Stand with feet hip-width apart, shoulders down and arms at your sides. Hinge forward from your hips and have your arms straight down towards the floor with your palms forward. Engage core.

Exhale, begin action by squeezing shoulder blades together and pull elbows up. Pause, **Inhale**, release. Repeat.

2. Triceps Kickbacks - 30 seconds' work/15 seconds' rest

Begin with left foot back and hinge forward from hips. Roll your shoulders back and bring elbows up just slightly higher than your torso.

Exhale, quickly extend arms out behind, making sure your shoulders don't roll forward and your elbows don't drop. **Inhale**, bend, keeping elbows still in space. Repeat.

3. Rear Delt Raises - 20 seconds' work/10 seconds' rest

Stand with feet hip-width apart, shoulders down and arms at your sides. Hinge forward from your hips and have arms straight down towards the floor with your palms turned towards the body. Engage core.

Exhale, pull elbows up and out to the sides. (Don't squeeze shoulder blades together.) Pause. **Inhale**, release. Repeat.

Notes:

_____

_____

_____

_____

_____

_____

_____

_____

1. Russian Twists - 40 seconds' work/20 seconds' rest

Sit tall on your *SITS bones, elbows in at sides, shoulders down, and legs together. Engage core and lean backwards, bringing legs up.

Exhale, twist torso to one side. **Inhale**, come back to centre. Repeat side 2 side.

*SITS bones = Ischial Tuberosity – the bony protrusions at the base of your pelvic bones.

2. Alternating Supine Obliques - 30 seconds' work/15 seconds' rest

Begin lying on your back with pelvis tilted (abs contracted) and legs together. Bring your hands behind your head and make your head very heavy. Lengthen the back of your neck (chin towards throat.)

Exhale, keeping elbows wide and pelvis stabilized with abs, quickly lift and twist left side of the ribcage to right hip (elbow and knee will align) **Inhale**, back to centre. Repeat side 2 side.

Modification: Begin with toes touching floor and alternate lifting knee.

3. Alternating Arm Reaches - 20 seconds' work/10 seconds' rest

Begin lying on your back with pelvis tilted and legs together. Engage your core, bring your hands behind your head, and make your head very heavy. Lengthen the back of your neck.

With exhalations, keeping elbows wide and pelvis stabilized with abs, quickly lift and twist, reaching left hand to the outside of right foot. Place hand behind head and repeat with the other side, bringing right hand to the outside of the left foot. Repeat side 2 side.

Modification: Bend legs.

Notes:

_____

_____

_____

_____

_____

_____

_____

_____

1. Plie Squats - 40 seconds' work/20 seconds' rest

Stand tall with legs turned out (knees in line with toes), abs connected, spine long.

Keeping shoulders rolled back and bringing your arms to the front, **inhale,** and lower down. **Exhale** and rise to standing. Repeat.

2. Plie Squats with DB Flyes - 30 seconds' work/15 seconds' rest

Stand tall with legs turned out (knees in line with toes), abs connected, spine long, and arms behind legs with palms facing forward.

Lower down into a plie squat. **Inhale** and raise arms to the front, bringing palms together. **Exhale** and take arms back. Repeat.

3. Plie Jumps - 20 seconds' work/10 seconds' rest

Stand tall with legs turned out (knees in line with toes), abs connected, and spine long. Place your weight down in front of you.

Inhale and <u>quickly</u> squat down and tap the weight. Exhale, jump! Repeat.

Notes:

_____

_____

_____

_____

_____

_____

_____

_____

1. Forearm Plank Holds - 40 seconds' work/20 seconds' rest

Begin lying prone on the mat with your knees down and wrap your hands around your elbows. Leave elbows where they are and, either bring your hands together in a prayer position or bring them in alignment with your elbows (shown). Push elbows outward to stabilize shoulders.

Engage your abs and lift knees off mat, straightening legs. Push your heels back and keep your body tight.

Challenge: Take your body lower!

2. Alternating Toe Taps - 30 seconds' work/15 seconds' rest

Engage your abs and lift knees off mat, straightening legs. Alternate tapping toes out to the side.

Modification: Begin with knees down, straightening leg as you tap toes.

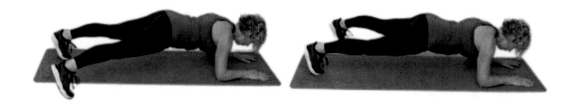

3. Double Knee Drops - 20 seconds' work/10 seconds' rest

Keep elbows under shoulders and hands flat on mat. Push elbows outward to stabilize shoulders.

Engage your abs and lift knees off mat, straightening legs.

Modification: Begin with knees down and straighten one leg at a time.
Challenge: Take your body lower!

Notes:

_____

_____

_____

_____

_____

_____

_____

WAIT TRAINING

Hold each stretch for 20-50 seconds

SIDE LYING BOW POSE x2

SWEET SPOT x2

BACK

HAMSTRINGS x2

HIP OPENER x2

CHEST OPENER

SIDE x2

WEEK 3 - DAY 1	DAY 2	DAY 3
Breakfast:	Breakfast:	Breakfast:
_____	_____	_____
_____	_____	_____
_____		
_____ Time:	_____ Time:	_____ Time:
Lunch:	Lunch:	Lunch:
_____	_____	_____
_____	_____	_____
_____ Time:	_____ Time:	_____ Time:
Snack:	Snack:	Snack:
_____	_____	_____
_____	_____	_____
_____ Time:	_____ Time:	_____ Time:
Dinner:	Dinner:	Dinner:
_____	_____	_____
_____	_____	_____
_____ Time:	_____ Time:	_____ Time:
Snack:	Snack:	Snack:
_____	_____	_____
_____	_____	_____
_____ Time:	_____ Time:	_____ Time:
Water: ⊔⊔⊔⊔⊔ ⊔⊔⊔⊔⊔	Water: ⊔⊔⊔⊔⊔ ⊔⊔⊔⊔⊔	Water: ⊔⊔⊔⊔⊔ ⊔⊔⊔⊔⊔
Today I am feeling:	**Today I am feeling:**	**Today I am feeling:**
_____	_____	_____
I am grateful for:	**I am grateful for:**	**I am grateful for:**
_____	_____	_____
_____	_____	_____
_____	_____	_____

DAY 4	DAY 5	DAY 6
Breakfast:	**Breakfast:**	**Breakfast:**
_____	_____	_____
_____	_____	_____
_____	_____	_____
_____ Time:	_____ Time:	_____ Time:
Lunch:	Lunch:	Lunch:
_____	_____	_____
_____	_____	_____
_____ Time:	_____ Time:	_____ Time:
Snack:	Snack:	Snack:
_____	_____	_____
_____	_____	_____
_____ Time:	_____ Time:	_____ Time:
Dinner:	Dinner:	Dinner:
_____	_____	_____
_____	_____	_____
_____ Time:	_____ Time:	_____ Time:
Snack:	Snack:	Snack:
_____	_____	_____
_____	_____	_____
_____ Time:	_____ Time:	_____ Time:

Water: ▽▽▽▽▽ ▽▽▽▽▽ (Day 4)
Water: ▽▽▽▽▽ ▽▽▽▽▽ (Day 5)
Water: ▽▽▽▽▽ ▽▽▽▽▽ (Day 6)

Today I am feeling: (Day 4)
_____
_____

Today I am feeling: (Day 5)
_____
_____

Today I am feeling: (Day 6)
_____
_____

I am grateful for: (Day 4)
_____
_____
_____

I am grateful for: (Day 5)
_____
_____
_____

I am grateful for: (Day 6)
_____
_____
_____

DAY 7 Total cups of water:	TOTAL CALORIES	FAT (g)	CHO (g)	PROTEIN (g)	Sodium (mg) < 2000 mg per day	Sugars (g) < 5g per day
BREAKFAST:						
SNACK:						
LUNCH:						
SNACK:						
DINNER:						
TOTALS:		x9	x4	x4		

Today I am feeling: _____

I am grateful for_____

WEEK THREE CHECK-IN

	Today's Date	Initial Assessment (page 68)	Difference
Blood Pressure			
Resting H.R.			
Weight			
Measurements			
Chest			
Waist			
Hips			
Right Arm			
Left Arm			
Right Thigh			
Right Calf			
Left Thigh			
Left Calf			
Total inches			

WINS: woohoo!!

1. _____

2. _____

3. _____

Adjustments to the program for the next three weeks:

1. _____

2. _____

3. _____

WEEK FOUR

My weekly goal is:

_____

To reach my goal, I will do these three things each day:

Sunday	Monday	Tuesday	Wednesday
Thursday	Friday	Saturday	

Daily Affirmation:

_____

_____

_____

HIIT 4

PERFORM 3X ALTERNATE DAYS IN THE WEEK

WARMUP: TOTAL: 4 minutes

1. ALT. STEP SIDE 2 SIDE

2. ALT. HAMSTRING CURLS

Exercises 1-8

Move 20-seconds / March10 seconds

3. ALT. KNEE LIFTS

4. ALT. SIDE REACHES

5. ALT. SHUFFLE SIDE 2 SIDE

----->   <-----

6. SKIPPING

7.   ALT. BOX TWISTS

8. ALT. HEEL DIGS

PUMP IT UP!

Three Exercises Per Body Part

40 seconds x3, rest 30 seconds.

Total time: 30 minutes

Equipment needed: Dumbbells

* CHOOSE A WEIGHT THAT CHALLENGES YOU AT 12 REPETITIONS

1. Sumo Squats/Curtsy Squats x2

2. Pullovers/One-arm Dumbbell Rows x2

3. Plie Squat Jumps/Lateral Lunges x2

4. Plie Squats with Dumbbell Flyes/Pushups/Plank Holds

5. Alternate Reverse Lunges/Lunge Twists x2

6. Shoulder Press Combos/Rear Delt Raises/Alternating Lateral and Anterior Raises

7. Leg Abductions, Right and Left/Good Mornings/Step Jumps

8. Triceps Pushups/Skull Crushers/Alternating Triceps Extensions

9. Standing Knee Lifts with a Twist x2/Plie Twists

10. Alternating Biceps Curls/Hammer Curls/Incline Biceps Curls

1. Sumo Squats – 40 seconds

Stand tall with feet shoulder-width apart, abs connected, spine long.
Inhale and squat down, keeping spine and neck in neutral.
Exhaling, tighten glutes and come to standing. Pause, repeat.

Curtsy Squats - 40 seconds, Right and Left

Begin standing with feet hip-width apart, shoulders down, and abs connected.
Inhale and squat, bringing right foot behind left in a curtsy manner. Exhale,
Stand. Repeat.

Perform same exercise with left foot coming behind.

30-SECOND REST

2. Pullovers - 40 seconds

Set up as shown with feet shoulder-width apart, pelvis tilted, abs connected, spine long. Use one weight or combine two together, as shown.

Inhale and without letting your back arch, lower straight arms behind head, keeping spine and neck in neutral.
Exhale, activate from around the under arms and pull arms forward. Pause, repeat.

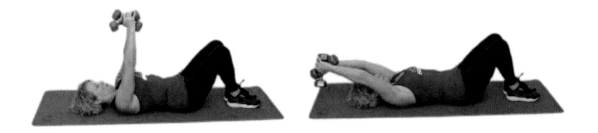

Standing Dumbbell Rows – 40 seconds, Right and Left

Begin with a split-stance, abs connected, spine long.

Inhale and squeeze right shoulder blade towards spine as you bring the elbow up, exhale, release. Repeat.

Repeat with the left side.

30-SECOND REST

3. Plie Squat Jumps - 40 seconds

Stand tall with legs turned out (knees in line with toes), abs connected, and spine long. Place your weight down in front of you.

Inhale and quickly squat down and tap the weight. Exhale and jump! Repeat.

Lateral Lunges – 40 seconds, Right and Left

Begin standing with feet hip-width apart, shoulders down, and abs connected. Inhale and squat to the left, bringing weights on either side of the foot. Exhale, Stand. Repeat.
Perform the exercise, squatting to the right.

30-SECOND REST

4. Plie Squats with Dumbbell Flyes - 40 seconds

Stand tall with legs turned out (knees in line with toes), abs connected, spine long, and arms behind legs with palms facing forward.

Lower down into a plie squat. **Inhale** and with a slight bend in the elbows, raise arms to the front, bringing palms together. **Exhale** and take arms back. Repeat.

Pushups - 40 seconds

Take hands wide (elbows should be over top of wrists at lowest point). Abs tight, shoulders down, and neck in line with spine.

Inhale and slowly BEND your elbows (the body and head will follow). ONLY GO AS LOW AS YOU CAN KEEP YOUR FORM.

Push back up and repeat.

Challenge:

Plank Holds – 40 seconds

Begin lying on mat with your knees down and wrap your hands around your elbows. Leave elbows where they are and either bring your hands together in a prayer position or bring them in alignment with your elbows (shown). Push elbows outward to stabilize shoulders.

Engage your abs and lift knees off mat, straightening legs. Push your heels back and keep your body tight.

Challenge 1: Take your body lower!
Challenge 2: Go into full plank.

30-SECOND REST

Notes:

_____

_____

_____

_____

_____

_____

_____

5. Alternate Reverse Lunges – 40 seconds

Stand tall with feet forward, abs connected, spine long, and arms at sides.

Inhale and step back, bending knees; pause. Exhale and come back up to standing. Continue exercise, alternating legs.

Lunge Twists - 40 seconds, Right and Left

Stand in a lunge position with left foot back, both feet and hips facing forward, shoulders down, abs tight. Hold a dumbbell between your hands at chest height.

Exhale as you slowly lower back knee towards the floor, pause and then twist upper body to the right. Return back to starting position. Repeat.

Repeat with right leg back, twisting to the left.

30-SECOND REST

6. Shoulder Press Combos – 40 seconds

Stand tall, abs connected, spine long, and palms in front of shoulders. Inhale, turn arms out to the sides, palms forward. Exhale, press arms up, inhale and bend elbows, exhale, bring back to starting position. Repeat.

Rear Delt Raises – 40 seconds

Stand with feet hip-width apart, shoulders down and arms at your sides. Hinge forward from your hips and have arms straight down towards the floor with your palms turned towards the body. Engage core.

Exhale, NOT squeezing shoulder blades together, pull elbows up and out to the sides. Pause, Inhale, release. Repeat.

Alternating Lateral and Anterior Raises – 40 seconds

Stand tall, abs connected, spine long, feet hip-width apart, and arms at your sides. Inhale.
Exhale, bring one arm straight up to the front, and one out to the side. Inhale, back to your sides. Exhale, repeat movement with the opposite arms. Repeat.

30-SECOND REST

Notes:

_____

_____

_____

_____

_____

_____

_____

_____

7. Leg Abductions, Right and Left – 15 reps on each leg

Stand tall with feet hip-width apart, abs connected, spine long, and hands on hips. Place your weight into your left leg and, from your hip, turn your right leg inward and tap foot out to the side.

Leading with your heel, **exhale,** and lift your leg up; pause. Inhale and come back up to standing. Repeat.

Perform exercise with the other leg.

Good Mornings – 40 seconds

Begin in posture, abs connected, spine long.
Inhale; hinge forward from hips, keeping spine in neutral. (don't bring your gaze forward!)
Exhale, tighten glutes and come to standing. Pause, and then repeat.

Alternating Lateral Step Jumps - 40 seconds

Jump side to side, tapping your foot as you land.

Challenge: Land on one foot without tapping down.

----->   <-----

30-SECOND REST

Notes:

_____

_____

_____

_____

_____

_____

_____

_____

8. Triceps Pushups – 40 seconds

Begin on all fours with wrists under shoulder, abs connected, spine long.

Inhale, slowly lower your body, bringing your chest down between your hands as you point your elbows back towards your feet. **Exhale,** push through arms to come back to start. Repeat.

Skull Crushers – 40 seconds

Set up as shown with feet shoulder-width apart, abs connected, spine long, and your hands above your shoulders.
Inhale, bend elbows and bring weights down beside your head, keeping elbows in line with your shoulders.
Exhale, Straighten your arms. Pause, repeat.

Alternating Triceps Extensions – 40 seconds

Stand with feet hip-width apart. Bend knees deeply, elbows at sides, palms in, abs connected, spine long.

Inhale and, simultaneously, slowly extend one arm straight out in front (turning palm down) and one back (turning palm up). **Exhale,** come back to start. Repeat, alternating front and back arms.

30-SECOND REST

Notes:

_____

_____

_____

_____

_____

_____

_____

_____

9. Standing Knee Lifts with Twists – 40 seconds, Right and Left

Stand with feet wide, shoulders down. Bring weight over to left shoulder, shifting weight to left foot.

Engage core, **exhale,** and twist to the right, simultaneously lifting right knee. **Inhale and release.** Repeat for 40 seconds.

 Repeat with right shoulder and left knee.

Alternating Plie Twists – 40 seconds

Stand in a plie squat position, knees and toes aligned; hold a weight between your hands, elbows at your sides and shoulders down.

Engage your core and with a pulsing **exhalation**, twist right and left, keeping head centre or moving it with the torso.

30-SECOND REST

10. Alternating Biceps Curls – 40 seconds

Stand with arms at sides, palms facing inwards, shoulders down, abs tight.

With a pulsing **exhalation,** bring one weight up and turn palm towards your shoulder. As you lower the weight, bring the other one up. Keep elbows close to sides. Repeat movements.

Hammer Curls – 40 seconds

Stand with arms at sides, palms facing inwards, shoulders down, abs tight.

Exhale, and bring both weights up to shoulders. **Inhale,** and lower. Keep elbows close to sides.

Incline Biceps Curls

Stand with feet hip-width apart and hinge forward from hips, allowing arms to hang below shoulders, palms facing forward, shoulders down and abs tight.

Exhale, keep elbows under shoulders and bring weights up to your forehead. Inhale, release. Repeat. (Do not move head towards weights!)

30-SECOND REST

Notes:

_____

_____

_____

_____

_____

_____

_____

_____

WAIT TRAINING

Hold each stretch for 20-50 seconds

CHEST OPENER   **HAMSTRINGS x2**   **HIP OPENER x2**

SIDE x2   **BACK**

SIDE LYING BOW POSE x2   **SWEET SPOT x2**

WEEK 4 - DAY 1

Breakfast:
_____
_____
_____ Time:

Lunch:
_____
_____
_____ Time:

Snack:
_____
_____
_____ Time:

Dinner:
_____
_____
_____ Time:

Snack:
_____
_____
_____ Time:

Water: ▽ ▽ ▽ ▽ ▽
       ▽ ▽ ▽ ▽ ▽

Today I am feeling:
_____
_____

I am grateful for:
_____
_____
_____

DAY 2

Breakfast:
_____
_____
_____ Time:

Lunch:
_____
_____
_____ Time:

Snack:
_____
_____
_____ Time:

Dinner:
_____
_____
_____ Time:

Snack:
_____
_____
_____ Time:

Water: ▽ ▽ ▽ ▽ ▽
       ▽ ▽ ▽ ▽ ▽

Today I am feeling:
_____
_____

I am grateful for:
_____
_____
_____

DAY 3

Breakfast:
_____
_____
_____ Time:

Lunch:
_____
_____
_____ Time:

Snack:
_____
_____
_____ Time:

Dinner:
_____
_____
_____ Time:

Snack:
_____
_____
_____ Time:

Water: ▽ ▽ ▽ ▽ ▽
       ▽ ▽ ▽ ▽ ▽

Today I am feeling:
_____
_____

I am grateful for:
_____
_____
_____

DAY 4

Breakfast:

_____
_____
_____
_____ Time: _____

Lunch:

_____
_____
_____ Time: _____

Snack:

_____
_____
_____ Time: _____

Dinner:

_____
_____
_____ Time: _____

Snack:

_____
_____
_____ Time: _____

Water: ☐ ☐ ☐ ☐ ☐
       ☐ ☐ ☐ ☐ ☐

Today I am feeling:

_____
_____

I am grateful for:

_____
_____
_____

DAY 5

Breakfast:

_____
_____
_____
_____ Time: _____

Lunch:

_____
_____
_____ Time: _____

Snack:

_____
_____
_____ Time: _____

Dinner:

_____
_____
_____ Time: _____

Snack:

_____
_____
_____ Time: _____

Water: ☐ ☐ ☐ ☐ ☐
       ☐ ☐ ☐ ☐ ☐

Today I am feeling:

_____
_____

I am grateful for:

_____
_____
_____

DAY 6

Breakfast:

_____
_____
_____
_____ Time: _____

Lunch:

_____
_____
_____ Time: _____

Snack:

_____
_____
_____ Time: _____

Dinner:

_____
_____
_____ Time: _____

Snack:

_____
_____
_____ Time: _____

Water: ☐ ☐ ☐ ☐ ☐
       ☐ ☐ ☐ ☐ ☐

Today I am feeling:

_____
_____

I am grateful for:

_____
_____
_____

Day 7 Total cups of water:	TOTAL CALORIES	FAT (g)	CHO (g)	PROTEIN (g)	Sodium (mg) < 2000 mg per day	Sugars (g) < 5g per day
BREAKFAST:						
SNACK:						
LUNCH:						
SNACK:						
DINNER:						
TOTALS:		x9	x4	x4		

Today I am feeling: _____

I am grateful for_____

WEEK FIVE

My weekly goal is:

_____

To reach my goal, I will do these three things each day:

Sunday	Monday	Tuesday	Wednesday
Thursday	Friday	Saturday	

Daily Affirmation:

_____

_____

_____

HIIT 5

WARMUP: TOTAL: 4 minutes

1. ALT. STEP SIDE 2 SIDE

2. ALT. HAMSTRING CURLS

Exercises 1-8

Perform each exercise for 30 seconds

3. ALT. KNEE LIFTS

4. ALT. SIDE REACHES

5. ALT. SHUFFLE SIDE 2 SIDE

----->   <-----

6. SKIPPING

7.   ALT. BOX TWISTS   8. ALT. HEEL DIGS

BODYWEIGHT HIIT

FULL BODY WORKOUT

Perform each exercise for 45seconds/rest 15 seconds.

Repeat 1x more

Total time: 25 minutes

Challenge: Repeat 1x more

No equipment needed

1. Reverse Lunge Taps/Knee Lifts, Left

2. Reverse Lunge Taps/Knee Lifts, Right

3. Alternating Supine Obliques

4. Push Ups

5. Alternating Lateral Step Jumps

6. Supported Alternating Can Cans

7. Reverse Lunge Knee Hops, Left

8. Reverse Lunge Knee Hops, Right

9. Side Plank Hold, Left

10. Side Plank Hold, Right

11. Skipping

12. Alternating Toe Taps

1. Reverse Lunge Tap/Knee Lifts – 45 seconds/rest 15 secs.

Begin with left foot back hinging from hips, feet hip-width apart and left arm forward.

Exhale, tap foot forward and back (double time) lifting the knee, making sure to change arms.

2. Repeat with the right foot back.

3. Alternating Supine Obliques – 45 seconds/rest 15 secs.

Begin lying on your back with pelvis tilted and legs together. Engage your core, bring your hands behind your head, and make your head very heavy. Lengthen the back of your neck.

Exhale, keeping elbows wide, and pelvis stabilized with abs, quickly lift and twist left ribcage to right hip (elbow and knee will align) **Inhale,** back to centre. Repeat side 2 side.

Modification: Begin with toes touching floor and alternate lifting knee.

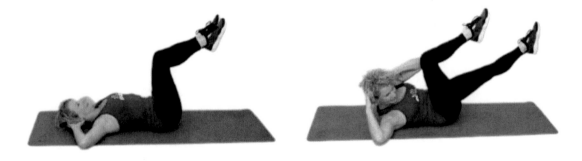

4. Pushups – 45 seconds/rest 15 secs.

Take hands wide (elbows should be over top of wrists at lowest point). Abs tight, shoulders down, and neck in line with spine.

Inhale and slowly BEND your elbows (the body and head will follow). ONLY GO AS LOW AS YOU CAN KEEP YOUR FORM.

Push back up and repeat.

CHALLENGE:

5. Alternating Lateral Step Jumps – 45 seconds/rest 15 secs.

Jump side to side, tapping your foot as you land.

Challenge: Land on one foot without tapping down.

----->   <-----

6. Supported Alternating Can Cans – 45 seconds/rest 15 secs.

Sit tall on your SITS bones, lean backwards onto your elbows, lift your chest, and pull your shoulders down. Bring your legs together, engage your core, and

one at a time, bring your legs up.

Exhale, twist torso to one side. Inhale, come back to centre. Repeat side 2 side.

7. Reverse Lunge Knee Hops – 45 seconds/rest 15 secs.

Begin with left foot back hinging from hips, feet hip-width apart and left arm forward. Lower your body down.

Exhaling, bring leg forward and hop, lifting knee, making sure to change arms. Inhale, bring foot back to the starting position.

8. Repeat with the right foot back.

9. Side Plank Hold, Left - 45 seconds/rest 15 secs.

Begin on your side, aligning bottom elbow under your shoulder, forearm forward, and your hips and feet in alignment with your elbow. Engage abs and lift your hip off the mat. Straighten your top arm.

Option 1: Lift top leg
Option 2: straighten both legs. Hold the position for 45 seconds.

10. Side Plank Hold, Right   - 45 seconds/rest 15 secs.

Notes:

_____

_____

_____

_____

_____

_____

_____

_____

11. Skipping – 45 seconds/rest 15 secs.

Imagine holding on to a skipping rope and begin to turn it from the movement at the shoulders.

Options:
Low impact: Keep toes on floor
Power jumping: Add a jump with each 'turn' of rope.

12. Alternating Toe Taps – 45 seconds/rest 15 secs.

Begin lying prone on the mat and place elbows under shoulders and hands flat on mat. Push elbows outward to stabilize shoulders.

Engage your abs and lift knees off mat, straightening legs. Alternate tapping toes out to the side.

Modification: Leave knees down, straightening leg as you tap toes.

One minute rest and then repeat series 1-12

WAIT TRAINING

Hold each stretch for 20-50 seconds

SIDE LYING BOW POSE x2

SWEET SPOT x2

BACK

HAMSTRINGS x2

HIP OPENER x2

SIDE x2

CHEST OPENER

WEEK 5 - DAY 1

Breakfast:
_____
_____
_____
_____ Time:

Lunch:
_____
_____
_____ Time:

Snack:
_____
_____
_____ Time:

Dinner:
_____
_____
_____ Time:

Snack:
_____
_____
_____ Time:

Water: ⑁ ⑁ ⑁ ⑁ ⑁
⑁ ⑁ ⑁ ⑁ ⑁

Today I am feeling:
_____
_____

I am grateful for:
_____
_____
_____

DAY 2

Breakfast:
_____
_____
_____ Time:

Lunch:
_____
_____
_____ Time:

Snack:
_____
_____
_____ Time:

Dinner:
_____
_____
_____ Time:

Snack:
_____
_____
_____ Time:

Water: ⑁ ⑁ ⑁ ⑁ ⑁
⑁ ⑁ ⑁ ⑁ ⑁

Today I am feeling:
_____
_____

I am grateful for:
_____
_____
_____

DAY 3

Breakfast:
_____
_____
_____ Time:

Lunch:
_____
_____
_____ Time:

Snack:
_____
_____
_____ Time:

Dinner:
_____
_____
_____ Time:

Snack:
_____
_____
_____ Time:

Water: ⑁ ⑁ ⑁ ⑁ ⑁
⑁ ⑁ ⑁ ⑁ ⑁

Today I am feeling:
_____
_____

I am grateful for:
_____
_____
_____

DAY 4

Breakfast:

_____
_____
_____ Time:

Lunch:

_____
_____
_____ Time:

Snack:

_____
_____
_____ Time:

Dinner:

_____
_____
_____ Time:

Snack:

_____
_____
_____ Time:

Water: ▽ ▽ ▽ ▽ ▽
       ▽ ▽ ▽ ▽ ▽

Today I am feeling:

_____
_____

I am grateful for:

_____
_____
_____

DAY 5

Breakfast:

_____
_____
_____ Time:

Lunch:

_____
_____
_____ Time:

Snack:

_____
_____
_____ Time:

Dinner:

_____
_____
_____ Time:

Snack:

_____
_____
_____ Time:

Water: ▽ ▽ ▽ ▽ ▽
       ▽ ▽ ▽ ▽ ▽

Today I am feeling:

_____
_____

I am grateful for:

_____
_____
_____

DAY 6

Breakfast:

_____
_____
_____ Time:

Lunch:

_____
_____
_____ Time:

Snack:

_____
_____
_____ Time:

Dinner:

_____
_____
_____ Time:

Snack:

_____
_____
_____ Time:

Water: ▽ ▽ ▽ ▽ ▽
       ▽ ▽ ▽ ▽ ▽

Today I am feeling:

_____
_____

I am grateful for:

_____
_____
_____

DAY 7 **Total cups of water:**	TOTAL CALORIES	FAT (g)	CHO (g)	PROTEIN (g)	Sodium (mg) < 2000 mg per day	Sugars (g) < 5g per day
BREAKFAST:						
SNACK:						
LUNCH:						
SNACK:						
DINNER:						
TOTALS:		x9	x4	x4		

Today I am feeling: _____

I am grateful for _____

WEEK SIX

My weekly goal is:

_____

To reach my goal, I will do these three things each day:

Sunday	Monday	Tuesday	Wednesday
Thursday	Friday	Saturday	

Daily Affirmation:

_____

_____

_____

HIIT 6

WARMUP: TOTAL: 4 minutes

1. ALT. STEP SIDE 2 SIDE

2. ALT. HAMSTRING CURLS

Exercises 1-8

Perform each exercise for 30 seconds

3. ALT. KNEE LIFTS

4. ALT. SIDE REACHES

5. ALT. SHUFFLE SIDE 2 SIDE

----->   <-----

6. SKIPPING

7. ALT. BOX TWISTS

8. ALT. HEEL DIGS

BOOTIE BURNER

Perform each exercise for 15 reps/rest 20 seconds.

Repeat once more.
Total time: 26 minutes

Equipment needed: Dumbbells

* CHOOSE A HEAVY WEIGHT THAT CHALLENGES YOU AT 12 REPETITIONS

1. Alternating Curtsy Squats

2. Good Mornings

3. Alternating Lateral Lunges

4. Sumo Squats

5. Alternating Reverse Lunges

6. Plie Squats

7. Balance Challenge

8. Leg Abductions, Right and Left

9. Bridge with Leg Lifts, Right and Left

1. Alternating Curtsy Squats – 30 reps' total

Begin standing with feet hip-width apart, shoulders down, and abs connected.
Inhale and squat, bringing right foot behind left in a curtsy manner. Exhale,
Stand.
Inhale and squat, bringing left foot behind right in a curtsy manner. Exhale,
Stand. Repeat side 2 side.

2. Good Mornings – 15 reps

Begin in posture, abs connected, spine long.
Inhale; hinge forward from hips, keeping spine in neutral.
Exhale, tighten glutes and come to standing. Pause, and then repeat.

3. Alternating Lateral Lunges – 30 reps' total

Begin in posture, abs connected, spine long.
Inhale: hinge sideways coming overtop of one knee, bringing weights on either side of the foot. Keep spine in neutral.
Exhale, come to standing. Pause, and then repeat to the other side.

4. Sumo Squats – 15 reps

Stand tall with feet shoulder-width apart, abs connected, spine long.
Inhale and squat down, keeping spine and neck in neutral.
Exhaling, tighten glutes and come to standing. Pause, repeat.

5. Alternating Reverse Lunges – 30 reps' total

Stand tall with feet forward, abs connected, spine long, and arms at sides.

Inhale and step back, bending knees; pause. **Exhale** and come back up to standing. Repeat stepping back with other leg and continuing alternating legs. .

6. Plie Squats - 15 reps

Stand tall with legs turned out (knees in line with toes), arms to the front, abs connected, and spine long.

Keeping shoulders rolled back, **inhale** and lower down. **Exhale** and rise to standing. Repeat.

7. Balance Challenge – Perform sequence 4x on each side

Stand tall with your feet hip-width apart, engage the core, and bring elbows to your sides with your hands in front of your chest.

1. **Inhale** and slowly lift your knee.

2. **Exhale,** slowly extend your arms upwards, and straighten your front leg.

3. **Inhale,** bend your elbows, bring your hands in front of your chest, and bend your knee.

4. **Exhale,** hinge from your hip, simultaneously pointing your hands down towards the floor and extending your leg behind you. (Allow your gaze to follow the movement of your body).

Bring your body back to the starting position.

Challenge: Hold a dumbbell between your hands.

8. Leg Abductions, Right and Left – 15 reps on each leg

Stand tall with feet hip-width apart, abs connected, spine long, and hands on hips. Place your weight in your left leg and, from your hip, turn your right leg inward and tap foot out to the side.

Leading with your heel, **exhale,** and lift your leg up; pause. Inhale, release. Repeat the 15 reps and come back to standing. Repeat on the other leg.

9. Bridge with Leg Lifts, Right and Left – 15 reps on each leg

Set up as shown with feet shoulder-width apart, pelvis in neutral, abs connected, spine long.
Inhale and press arms and feet into the floor, connecting back muscles and feeling the glutes. **Exhale** and lift hips. Bring left knee in towards chest and straighten leg. With **exhalation** pulses, press foot up to the ceiling for 15 reps. Lower body to floor and repeat with the other leg.

WAIT TRAINING

Hold each stretch for 20-50 seconds

SIDE LYING BOW POSE x2

SWEET SPOT x2

BACK

HAMSTRINGS x2

HIP OPENER x2

SIDE x2

CHEST OPENER

WEEK 6 - DAY 1

Breakfast:

_____
_____
_____
_____ Time:

Lunch:

_____
_____
_____ Time:

Snack:

_____
_____
_____ Time:

Dinner:

_____
_____
_____ Time:

Snack:

_____
_____
_____ Time:

Water: ▽ ▽ ▽ ▽ ▽
▽ ▽ ▽ ▽ ▽

Today I am feeling:

_____
_____

I am grateful for:

_____
_____
_____

DAY 2

Breakfast:

_____
_____
_____ Time:

Lunch:

_____
_____
_____ Time:

Snack:

_____
_____
_____ Time:

Dinner:

_____
_____
_____ Time:

Snack:

_____
_____
_____ Time:

Water: ▽ ▽ ▽ ▽ ▽
▽ ▽ ▽ ▽ ▽

Today I am feeling:

_____
_____

I am grateful for:

_____
_____
_____

DAY 3

Breakfast:

_____
_____
_____ Time:

Lunch:

_____
_____
_____ Time:

Snack:

_____
_____
_____ Time:

Dinner:

_____
_____
_____ Time:

Snack:

_____
_____
_____ Time:

Water: ▽ ▽ ▽ ▽ ▽
▽ ▽ ▽ ▽ ▽

Today I am feeling:

_____
_____

I am grateful for:

_____
_____
_____

DAY 4	DAY 5	DAY 6
Breakfast:	Breakfast:	Breakfast:

DAY 4

Breakfast:

_____

_____

_____

_____ Time:

Lunch:

_____

_____

_____

_____ Time:

Snack:

_____

_____

_____

_____ Time:

Dinner:

_____

_____

_____

_____ Time:

Snack:

_____

_____

_____

_____ Time:

Water: ▽ ▽ ▽ ▽ ▽
▽ ▽ ▽ ▽ ▽

Today I am feeling:

_____

_____

I am grateful for:

_____

_____

_____

DAY 5

Breakfast:

_____

_____

_____

_____ Time:

Lunch:

_____

_____

_____

_____ Time:

Snack:

_____

_____

_____

_____ Time:

Dinner:

_____

_____

_____

_____ Time:

Snack:

_____

_____

_____

_____ Time:

Water: ▽ ▽ ▽ ▽ ▽
▽ ▽ ▽ ▽ ▽

Today I am feeling:

_____

_____

I am grateful for:

_____

_____

_____

DAY 6

Breakfast:

_____

_____

_____

_____ Time:

Lunch:

_____

_____

_____

_____ Time:

Snack:

_____

_____

_____

_____ Time:

Dinner:

_____

_____

_____

_____ Time:

Snack:

_____

_____

_____

_____ Time:

Water: ▽ ▽ ▽ ▽ ▽
▽ ▽ ▽ ▽ ▽

Today I am feeling:

_____

_____

I am grateful for:

_____

_____

_____

DAY 7 Total cups of water:	TOTAL CALORIES	FAT (g)	CHO (g)	PROTEIN (g)	Sodium (mg) < 2000 mg per day	Sugars (g) < 5g per day
BREAKFAST:						
SNACK:						
LUNCH:						
SNACK:						
DINNER:						
TOTALS:		x9	x4	x4		

Today I am feeling: _____

I am grateful for_____

WEEK SIX CHECK-IN

	Today's Date	Initial Assessment (page 68)	Difference
Blood Pressure			
Resting H.R.			
Weight			
Measurements			
Chest			
Waist			
Hips			
Right Arm			
Left Arm			
Right Thigh			
Right Calf			
Left Thigh			
Left Calf			
Total inches			

GOALS ACCOMPLISHED...

FITNESS: _____

_____

HEALTH:_____

_____

WELLNESS:_____

_____

YOU ARE AMAZING, BEAUTIFUL, BRAVE,
AND A LIGHT TO THIS WORLD.

KEEP SHINING BRIGHTLY!

Notes:

PILATES ON THE STABILITY BALL

WHAT SIZE STABILITY BALL SHOULD YOU USE?

When choosing a stability ball, you want a size relative to your height. When you sit on the ball, with your feet flat on the floor and your spine is tall (ribs stacked over hips), your legs should be at a 90-degree angle or slightly more, but not less.

Person's height:

4'6" to 5' tall	45 cm ball
5' to 5'5" tall	55 cm ball
5'6" to 6'2" tall	65 cm ball
➢ 6'2" tall	75 cm ball

Roll Down

Sit tall and engage your core. **Inhale,** lengthen the back of your neck, and leading with the crown of your head, **exhale** and roll your body down, letting your arms slide down the front of your legs.
Inhale, pause; **exhale,** roll back up again, stacking your spine one vertebra at a time. Repeat 4x.

Leg Lifts

Continue engaging your core and gently hold the ball with your fingertips (as shown.)
Inhale, exhale, and slowly extend the leg, gliding your foot off the floor. Keep the knee lifted; lower and raise the lower leg. Repeat 8x and then switch legs.

Alternate Arm Raises

Inhale, raise one arm out to the side (palm up), and **exhale** as you slowly lean to one side (try to keep the ball still). Inhale, raise the arm to the ceiling, **exhale**, and return the hand to the ball. Repeat on the other side and then alternate sides for a total of 10x.

Walkouts

Begin sitting tall and engage your core. Inhale and walk your feet forward, scooping your abs as you let your body roll down the ball. **Exhale**, engage your abs and roll back up to sitting. Repeat 4x

Neutral Spine

Place your back flat on the mat and put your legs on the ball. Make a triangle with your index fingers and thumbs, and place your hands on your pelvis. (Your fingers will be higher than your thumbs).

Tilt your pelvis toward your feet until your fingers and thumbs are on the same horizontal plane and your lower back is off the floor. This position is your neutral spine.

Bridges 1/2

Place your lower legs on the ball. (The further away the ball is from the body, the more challenging the work.) The spine is neutral, and your arms are long at your sides. **Inhale**, lengthen your neck, **exhale**, push through your arms and heels, and lift your hips off the floor. **Inhale**, hold, **exhale**, lower hips. Repeat 5x

Bridges 2/2

Place your feet on the ball and begin in neutral; press down through your arms. Exhale, use abs to tip pelvis (tilt), and roll the spine off the mat one vertebra at a time. Inhale, hold at the top, exhale, and roll the spine back down through to neutral. Repeat 3x

Alternating Can Cans

Anchor your arms to the floor. Lengthen the back of the neck and use your abs to tip the pelvis gently. Inhale and roll the ball to the right; exhale and move the ball back to the centre. Repeat, alternating side to side 4x.

Challenge: Straighten the legs when rolling the ball out to the side.

Spine Extensions

Begin lying over the ball, neck in neutral, hands gently touching the ball, and your feet as wide as you need them to be for stability. **Exhale** and pully belly towards the spine. **Inhale**, slide shoulders down, engage your upper back, lift into extension, exhale, and lower. Repeat 6x

Challenge: Reach arms up as you come into the extension

Alternating Arm and Leg Balances

Move the ball under you so that you can balance through your hands and feet. Place legs in a wide stance. Pull your belly to the spine and tighten up your waist muscles. **Inhale** to prepare for movement, **exhale** and glide the opposite arm and leg up and out to the side. **Inhale,** bring it back to the floor and, **exhale,** raise the other arm and leg. Repeat 16x total.

Alternating One Leg Kicks

Begin on the top of the ball with wrists under shoulders and leg out straight, glutes contracted. With a pulsing breath, **exhale** and flex the foot, **exhale** and point the foot, and **inhale** to lower. Switch legs and repeat. Total 12x

Pushups

Place the ball under you, from your hips to your toes (the further the ball is away from the hands, the more challenging the exercise). Maintain a neutral spine and stabilize your shoulder blades. **Inhale** and bend elbows over the top of the wrists, **exhale**, engage the chest and push up. (Neck and legs stay in alignment with torso). Repeat 10x

Rollouts

Set up as shown, spine neutral, core engaged, arms strong, and baby fingers touching the ball. **Inhale** as you roll the ball away, letting your whole body move. **Exhale** and pull the ball in, tightening the core and returning to starting position. (Don't lead back with your glutes!) Repeat 8x

Half Pikes

Set up with the ball under your knees and wrists under your shoulders. Engage core. **Exhale,** pull the ball into your chest by contracting your abs, keeping your glutes lifted and neck in alignment with your spine. **Inhale** back to the start. Repeat 8x

Cat/Cow Stretches

Begin kneeling tall behind the ball with palms facing in. Inhale, push the ball away, keeping hips over knees. Exhale, engage the core, and round back into a cat stretch. Repeat moves 5x

Situps

Sit on top of the ball and walk your feet out until the ball is in the small of your back; place your hands behind your head. Drop your pelvis BUT don't tuck it. Inhale, lean back over the ball, exhale, and curl up. Repeat 5x

On the next rep, alternate reaching hand to opposite knee. Repeat a total of 10x

Leg Abductions

Place the ball between the legs. Engage your core and tilt your spine towards the floor. **Exhale,** keeping your legs straight, split them and catch the ball. **Inhale,** throw the ball up, and catch it between the legs. Repeat 8-10x

Alternate Arm and Leg Reaches

Hold the ball between your fingers and toes. The spine is neutral, and the core is engaged. **Inhale,** keeping the legs and arms straight, and reach the opposite arm and leg away. **Exhale,** bring back to the ball. Repeat the movement with the other arm and leg. Continue alternating for a total of 12x

Rollovers

Place the ball between your ankles and use your abs to tilt the pelvis to the mat. Lengthen the back of the neck, shoulders down, with your arms at your sides. Inhale, and slowly move your legs towards your chest. Exhale, engage your core, push your arms down, and take your legs over your head, bringing the ball to the floor. Inhale, bring your legs to parallel, exhale and slowly roll your spine back down. Repeat 5x.

Teasers

Place the ball under your feet and use your abs to tilt the pelvis to the mat. Lengthen the back of the neck, shoulders down, with your arms at your sides. Inhale, and raise your arms. Exhale, engage your core, lift your upper body off the floor, and push the ball away. Inhale, raise your arms, exhale, and roll your spine back down, pulling the ball back to the starting position. Repeat 5x.

TIME TO STRETCH

Body Twists

Place the ball under your left leg and roll it to the left. 'Snug" your right leg into the ball. Take your arms into a 'T' position, anchor your shoulders, engage your core, and roll the ball over the right leg. Hold for 20 seconds, and then repeat on the other side.

Lower Back Stretches

Sit on top of the ball with your legs wide. Engage your core, hinge from your hips, and bring your hands to the floor. Hold for 10 seconds.

Slowly walk your hands over to the right, taking your left hand to the outside of your right foot. Roll the ball to the left and hold for 15 seconds. Walk your hands over to your left foot. Grab it with your right hand and roll the ball to the right. Hold for 15 seconds.

Seated Twists

Sit tall on the ball with your feet wide. Take your right hand to the outside of your left knee and place your left hand behind on the ball.

Exhale and twist, using the leg as a lever. Hold the stretch for 10 seconds, then repeat on the other side.

Side Stretches

Sit tall on the ball and engage your core. Inhale, raise your right arm out to the side (palm up), exhale, and lean to the left, rolling the ball to the right and sliding your left hand down the ball. Hold for 10 seconds. Inhale and come back to the centre. Repeat on the other side.

Hip Extensions

Stand in a lunge position with the ball on the outside of the front (left) leg. Roll the ball under the front leg and sit on the ball (feet should be hip-width apart, and your back heel should be lifted). Tighten your right glute and push the ball forward with your right leg.

Keeping the left hand on the ball, raise the right arm, and reach backward. Feel the stretch up the right side of the body. Hold for 10-20 seconds, then repeat on the other side.

Notes:

_____

_____

_____

_____

_____

_____

_____

_____

DELICIOUS RECIPES
For The bodyFIT Program

BREAKFAST
Baked Apple Pancake
Banana Cookies
Banana Protein Pancake
Cheesy Zucchini & Carrot Squares
Egg Tortilla Breakfast Wrap
Pumpkin Cranberry Granola Bars

LUNCH
Chicken Lettuce Wraps
Chopped Greek Salad for two
Crustless Spinach, Onion & Feta Quiche
Curried Potato and Cauliflower
Italian Chicken Tomato Bean Soup
Roasted Yam & Chicken Salad

DINNER
Beef n' Broccoli
Chili Lime Sweet Potato Salad
Fish Tacos
Margarita Spaghetti Squash
Salmon Sashimi
Tenderloin Fajita Wraps

TREAT DAY DELIGHTS
Amazing Coconut Oil Fudge
Chocolate Avocado Mousse
Chunky Delight Granola Bars
Lara Bars
Sexy Black Rice Pudding
Yummy Muffins

BREAKFAST

Baked Apple Pancake

1 tsp butter or plant-based
1 tsp brown sugar
1 tsp white sugar
¾ tsp ground cinnamon
1 large cooking apple or 2 mediums, cored and sliced

1 large egg + 4 egg whites
¼ cup skim milk
¼ cup all-purpose flour

Preheat oven to 375°. Melt margarine over medium heat in an 8–10-inch frying or omelet pan with an ovenproof handle*. Stir in brown and white sugars and cinnamon. Arrange apple slices in a single layer over the sugar mixture in a pinwheel design. Cook, turning the slices occasionally until tender but firm, about 3-4 minutes. Mix remaining ingredients until smooth; pour over apple slices. Bake until golden brown (approx. 15 minutes.) Serve immediately.

*To make the handle ovenproof, wrap it completely with aluminum foil.

Banana Cookies

3 bananas, mashed
2 cups quick-cooking oatmeal
½ cup raisins
1/3 cup apple sauce
¼ cup almond milk
1 tsp. each vanilla and cinnamon

Preheat oven to 350°. Spray a cookie sheet with cooking oil.
Mix all ingredients and scoop a ¼ cup mixture onto the cookie sheet for each cookie, 1 inch apart, and slightly flatten with a fork.

Bake for 15-20 minutes. Remove and cool on a wire rack. These cookies are a great on-the-go breakfast!

Banana Protein Pancake

2 large eggs OR 6 egg whites
1 cup oats, grounded
1 cup light Cottage Cheese, blended smooth
½ tsp. Cinnamon
½ tsp. Vanilla
¼ tsp. baking powder
1 small banana, smashed

Mix all the ingredients in a blender or medium mixing bowl.
Preheat a skillet to medium heat. Pour in ¼ cup of the mixture (per pancake) and cook until lightly brown.

Cheesy Zucchini & Carrot Squares

4 medium-large zucchinis, grated
Salt
2 large carrots, grated
1 tbsp. olive oil
4 large free-range eggs
¾ cup Jarlsberg, Swiss, or Edam cheese, shredded
3 tbsp. parmesan cheese, grated
3 tbsp. Dry-roasted sunflower seeds

¼ cup parsley, chopped
2 green onions, chopped
1 clove garlic, minced

Preheat oven to 350°– lightly grease an 11x7" baking dish. Place grated zucchini in a colander and lightly salt. Let the zucchini rest for 15 mins. Squeeze out the moisture from the zucchini until quite dry. Pat the grated carrot dry.
Heat oil in a large skillet over medium heat. Add zucchini and carrot, and sauté until crisp-tender. Meanwhile, in a medium-sized bowl, beat eggs lightly. Mix in the cheese of your choice, parsley, green onions, garlic, basil, and sauteed veggies. Place the mixture in the baking dish.

Sprinkle the top with parmesan cheese and sunflower seeds. Bake for 30 minutes or until the filling is set. Remove from oven and cool slightly for a minute or two before cutting it into squares. It can be served hot or cold.

Egg Tortilla Breakfast Wrap

Oil spray
1 medium tortilla wrap
2 eggs
1 tbsp. Water
Seasonings of your choice (optional)

Wrap Fixins

¼ avocado, sliced
½ cup fresh spinach
1 tbsp. grated mozzarella cheese
1 tbsp. feta cheese
Fried onions and peppers

Use a frying pan (to fit the size of your tortilla wrap). Spray the frying pan with oil and heat (medium heat). Beat together the eggs and milk/cream in a bowl. Add seasonings. Pour in pan and cook until egg has cooked 1/2 way, lifting edges of uncooked egg to seep under.

Turn down the heat to med/low. Place the tortilla on top of the egg, ensuring the two adhere. Flip the tortilla over (the omelet is on top).

Load up your wrap with the fixins of your choice. Slide wrap onto a plate and fold into thirds. Serve with low-fat sour cream.

Pumpkin Cranberry Granola Bars

¼ cup coconut oil
1 cup old-fashioned rolled oats
1 cup quick-cooking oats
2/3 cup dried cranberries
2/3 cup pumpkin seeds
¼ cup ground flax

1 tsp. pumpkin pie spice
½ tsp. sea salt
½ cup pumpkin puree
2 eggs, beaten
¼ cup honey

Preheat oven to 350°. Cover a baking sheet with parchment paper; set aside. In a large bowl, melt the coconut oil in the microwave.

Combine the oats (x2), cranberries, pumpkin seeds, flax, pumpkin pie spice, and salt in a medium size bowl. Mix the dry ingredients into the coconut oil, then add pumpkin puree and beaten eggs; mix well.

Scoop ¼ cup of mixture onto the baking tray and flatten each scoop with a fork, creating a rectangular shape. Bake for 15-20 minutes and let cool on a wire rack.

Your favourite recipes:

_____

_____

_____

_____

_____

_____

_____

_____

_____

_____

_____

_____

_____

_____

_____

_____

_____

LUNCH

Chicken Lettuce Wraps

1 lb. ground chicken
1 tbsp. Olive oil
2 cloves garlic, minced
1 onion, chopped
¼ cup hoisin sauce
1 tbsp. Low sodium soy sauce
1 tbsp. Rice wine vinegar

1 tbsp. freshly grated ginger
1 tsp. sriracha, optional
1 8-oz. can of water chestnuts, drained/diced
2 green onions, thinly sliced
Salt and freshly ground black pepper to taste
1 head lettuce, butter, iceberg, or romaine.

Heat oil in a saucepan over medium heat. Add ground chicken and cook until browned, about 5-7 minutes, crumbling chicken as it cooks. Drain off excess fat.

Stir in garlic, onion, hoisin sauce, soy sauce, rice wine vinegar, ginger, and sriracha sauce, and cook until the onions become translucent.

Stir in chestnuts and green onions, cooking until tender, about 1-2 minutes; season with salt and pepper to taste. To serve, spoon several tbsps. of the chicken mixture into the centre of a lettuce leaf, taco-style.

Chopped Greek Salad for two

2 ½ tbsp. red-wine vinegar
1 tbsp. extra-virgin olive oil
1 ½ tsp. chopped fresh dill, or ½ tsp. dried
½ tsp. garlic powder
1/8th tsp. each of salt and freshly ground pepper
3 cups chopped romaine lettuce
1 ¼ cups chopped cooked chicken
1 medium tomato, chopped
½ medium cucumber, peeled, seeded, and chopped

¼ cup finely chopped red onion
¼ cup sliced ripe black olives
¼ cup crumbled feta cheese

Whisk vinegar, oil, dill, garlic powder, salt, and pepper in a large bowl. Add lettuce, chicken, tomato, cucumber, onion, olives, and feta; toss to coat.

Garlic-Tomato Toasts

2 slices whole-wheat country bread
1 small clove garlic, cut in half
½ tsp. Extra-virgin olive oil

1 small plum tomato, cut in half
Salt and pepper to taste

Grill or toast the bread. Rub one side with the cut side of the garlic clove half and drizzle with the olive oil. Rub with the cut side of the tomato half. Sprinkle with salt and pepper.

Crustless Spinach, Onion & Feta Quiche

1 tbsp. olive oil
1 medium onion, diced
6 oz. fresh baby spinach

2 large eggs, and 2 large egg whites
½ cup all-purpose flour
½ tsp. baking powder
¼ tsp. salt
Pinch cayenne pepper
1 1/3 cups skim or plant-based milk
½ cup feta cheese

Preheat oven to 400°. Lightly grease a 10-inch quiche/tart pan or pie plate. Put oil in a medium frying pan and cook onion over medium-high heat until translucent and tender. Add in spinach and cook until just wilted. Set aside to cool for a few minutes.

Mix eggs, flour, baking powder, and salt in a medium bowl. Whisk in milk, and then stir in the spinach-onion mixture. Pour ingredients into the prepared pan. Top with feta cheese.

Bake for 25 minutes until the centre is set and the outside edge is golden brown. Let sit for 5 minutes, then slice and serve.

Curried Potato and Cauliflower

2 tbsp. olive oil
1 large onion, diced large
2 tsp. curry powder (or less/more to your liking)
1-2 tbsp. water
1 large potato, diced
2 cups cauliflower florets
1 cup water
Salt and pepper, to taste

Heat olive oil in a medium skillet over medium heat and add the onions—Sauté for approximately 5 minutes or until the onions are soft.

Sprinkle the curry powder over the onions, stirring constantly for 2-3 minutes. Add the water to avoid scorching the powder.

Add all the other ingredients, cover, and simmer for 15-20 minutes, stirring occasionally, until the vegetables are cooked. Serve with your favourite protein.

Italian Chicken Tomato Bean Soup

1 lb. chicken breasts, cut into 1-inch cubes
2-14 oz. cans red beans
2-14 oz. cans white beans
28 oz. can crushed tomatoes
4 cups low-sodium vegetable broth
2 large potatoes, diced
2 cups diced carrots

1 medium zucchini, sliced
1 medium yellow squash, diced
½ cup chopped onion
1 tbsp. dried basil
¼ tsp. black pepper
1 clove garlic, minced

Combine all into a crockpot and cook on low heat for 6 hours **or** place in pot on the stove, bring to a boil, and then simmer, covered, for 45 minutes to 1 hour.

Roasted Yam & Chicken Salad

1 1lb chicken breasts, skinless and boneless
3 cups yam, peeled and cubed
½ cup grapeseed oil
Salt and pepper to taste
¼ cup dried cranberries
½ cup whole almonds, roasted
¼ cup green onion, finely sliced
½ cup cilantro, roughly chopped

Dressing
¼ cup light coconut milk
¼ cup rice vinegar
¼ cup fresh lime juice
1-2 tsp. curry spice blend
1 tsp. Dijon mustard
1 clove garlic, minced
1 tsp fresh ginger, minced
¾ cup grapeseed oil

Preheat oven to 350°. Toss chicken in ¼ cup oil and season with salt and pepper. Lay on a parchment-lined cookie sheet and roast for 25 minutes. Cool and then chop into cubes.

Toss yam in ¼ cup oil, season with salt and pepper, and lay on **another** parchment-lined cookie sheet. Roast for 30-40 minutes until cooked.

Mix the dried cranberries, almonds, green onions, and cilantro with the chicken and yam in a large bowl.

Dressing: In a blender, place coconut milk, rice vinegar, lime juice, curry spice blend, Dijon mustard, garlic, and ginger. Puree until smooth. Slowly add the oil while blending until the dressing thickens.

Toss salad with dressing; serve warm.

Your favourite recipes:

_____

_____

_____

_____

_____

_____

_____

_____

_____

_____

_____

_____

_____

_____

_____

_____

_____

DINNER

Beef n' Broccoli
1 Steak, thinly sliced across grain
¼ tsp. pepper
1 tbsp. oil

¾ cup water
1 tbsp. oyster sauce
1 tbsp. cornstarch

1 tbsp. oil
4 cups broccoli
2 cloves garlic, minced
1 tbsp. ginger, minced

Mix the water, oyster sauce, and cornstarch in a small bowl; set aside.

Heat the 1st amount of oil in a wok over medium/high heat. Sprinkle steak with pepper, add to oil, and stir-fry until browned (approx. 3 minutes); transfer to a plate.

Heat 2nd amount of oil. Add broccoli, garlic, and ginger. Stir-fry for 1 minute at med-high heat, cover, and steam for 2 minutes.

Return the beef to the wok. Add the oyster sauce mixture. Stir-fry all the ingredients for approx. three minutes until sauce thickens. Serve with rice.

Chili Lime Sweet Potato Salad
2lbs yams peeled and cubed
1 of each red and yellow pepper

Dressing
1/3 cup olive oil
1 ½ tbsp. chili powder,
1 tsp. ground cumin
4 tbsp. lime juice

4 green onions, sliced
¼ cup fresh cilantro, roughly chopped

Preheat oven to 400°. Spray a baking tray or roasting pan with cooking oil. Make the dressing and set aside in a medium-sized bowl. Toss together the yams and peppers and bake for 25-30 minutes.

Add the yams and peppers to the bowl with the dressing; toss and place back onto the baking tray. Cook for another 30 minutes or more until the veggies are cooked through. Place the veggies back into the bowl and toss in the green onions and cilantro. Serve at room temperature with a protein of your choice.

Fish Tacos

1 lb. white fish fillet, cut into 1 1/2 " strips
1 tsp. paprika
½ tsp. garlic powder
¼ tsp. oregano
¼ tsp. thyme
¼ tsp. ground pepper
¼ tsp. salt
1/8th tsp. cayenne
2 tbsp. vegetable oil
2 tbsp. lemon juice
1 package of taco shells or flour tortillas

Toppings
Shredded cabbage
Tomatoes, chopped
Lime wedges
Cilantro, roughly chopped

Avocado Crema
1 avocado, mashed
2 tbsp. fresh lime juice
¼ cup cilantro, roughly chopped
½ jalapeno, diced into small pieces
½ tsp. salt
1-2 tbsp. water

Crema: Combine all the ingredients in a food processor and puree until smooth. Set aside.

Mix the paprika, garlic powder, oregano, thyme, ground pepper, salt, and cayenne in a small bowl.

Combine the fish, vegetable oil, and lemon juice in a medium bowl. Add the spices. Pour into a large skillet. Cook on medium-high heat, stirring constantly, for 4-5 minutes or until fish flakes easily when tested with a fork.

Place fish in taco shells. Top with crema and toppings of your choice.

Margarita Spaghetti Squash

1 large spaghetti squash
2 tbsp. olive oil
1 tsp. each of salt, pepper, and garlic powder
1 large Roma tomato, finely chopped
¼ cup shredded mozzarella cheese
2 tbsp. finely chopped basil

Preheat oven to 375°. Prepare the squash by pulling out the seeds, and with pulp side up, drizzle with olive oil, salt, pepper, and garlic powder. Place the pulp side down onto a cookie sheet, and bake for 30-40 minutes, checking for doneness. Once the squash is cooked, scrape the pulp with a fork and leave it in the skin.

Set the oven to broil. While heating the oven, sprinkle both squash pieces with the chopped tomato and basil. Top with cheese and broil for 3-4 minutes.

Allow to cool for 5 minutes before serving.

Salmon Sashimi

6-7 oz. fresh salmon fillet
Oil

Rub Mix
1 tbsp. ground ginger
1 tbsp. paprika
1 tsp. onion powder
1 tsp. garlic powder
1 tsp. cayenne
¾ tsp. each of white and black pepper
½ tsp. thyme leaves
½ tsp. oregano leaves
½ tsp. parsley flakes

Sides
Fresh lemon wedges
Pickled Ginger
Wasabi
Low sodium soy sauce

Lightly oil the salmon fillet and season on both sides with the rub mixture. Barbeque on high heat in a cast iron pan. Sear salmon, turning once, and cook to medium rare. Let the fish cool in the fridge, slice it thinly, and serve with salad or rice.

Tenderloin Fajita Wraps

1 large yellow or orange pepper, sliced into thin strips
1 large onion, sliced into thin strips
1 pork tenderloin, sliced into bite-size strips
2 tsp. olive oil
2 tsp. dried oregano
1 tsp each of chili powder, garlic salt, and Tabasco sauce
½ cup salsa

6-8 medium tortilla wraps
Lettuce leaves
Low-fat sour cream

Pour oil into a large frying pan or wok and heat to medium-high. Add the pork and stir-fry until it loses its pink colour, about 3 minutes. Push to the edge of the pan.

Reduce heat to medium and add pepper and onion. Stir the vegetables often until the onion is soft, 4 to 5 minutes. Sprinkle with oregano, chili powder, garlic salt, and Tabasco. Add the salsa and stir for 1 to 2 minutes. Add more salt to taste.

Spread sour cream onto the tortilla wrap, and top it with lettuce, pork, and veggies. Serve with extra salsa.

Your favourite recipes:

_____

_____

_____

_____

_____

_____

_____

_____

_____

_____

_____

_____

_____

_____

_____

_____

_____

_____

TREAT DAY DELIGHTS

Amazing Coconut Oil Fudge

1 cup coconut oil, solid but not cold
¼ cup whole coconut milk
¼ to ½ cup cocoa powder
¼ cup raw honey
1 tsp. vanilla extract
½ tsp. almond extract

Place a sheet of parchment or wax paper along the bottom of a loaf pan, making sure to have at least 4" of the piece hanging over both short edges of the pan, creating 'handles.'

In a medium bowl, combine the coconut oil and milk with a stand mixer or hand mixer on medium-high and beat the milk and oil together for 5-6 minutes until it is glossy and thick. Add the remaining ingredients to the mixer and mix on low until the cocoa is incorporated. Mix on high until the mixture is smooth and thoroughly combined.

Pour the chocolate mixture into the prepared pan and smooth it out with the back of a spoon—place in the freezer for about 20 minutes until just set.

Pull the fudge from the pan by grabbing the 'handles' and laying it on a cutting board. Peel off the paper and flip the fudge. Use a sharp knife to cut the fudge into small squares. Store in an airtight container in the freezer.

Chocolate Avocado Mousse

1 ripe avocado
¼ cup cocoa powder
¼ cup raw agave nectar/honey
¼ cup almond milk
1 tsp. vanilla

Remove the pit of the avocado and place the avocado flesh in a blender. Add the rest of the ingredients and puree until smooth. Transfer to serving dish and place in refrigerator until chilled, about one hour.

Chunky Delight Granola Bars

1 cup packed Medjool dates, pitted
¼ cup maple or agave syrup
¼ cup creamy natural peanut or almond butter
1 cup roasted unsalted almonds, loosely chopped
1 ½ cups rolled oats

Additions
Nuts
Banana chips
Vanilla extract
Dried fruit
Dried cranberries

Place a piece of parchment or waxed paper over the bottom of an 8x8" baking dish, making sure to have at least 4" hanging over the sides of the dish creating "handles."

Process the dates in a food processor until small bits remain and a "dough-like" consistency is formed. Mix the dates, almonds, and oats in a medium bowl together, breaking up the dates so they are dispersed throughout the mixture. Set aside.

Warm the syrup and nut butter over low heat in a small saucepan, stirring continuously. When combined, pour over the date mixture and blend all ingredients.

Transfer the mixture to the baking dish and press down until uniformly flattened. Cover with plastic wrap and set in the freezer for 20 minutes to harden.

Remove the mixture from the pan and chop it into 10 bars. Store the bars in an airtight container in the freezer. The bars do not freeze and are ready to eat!

Lara Bars

16 dates (process in hot water if you need to soften)
3 cups walnuts
1 cup coconut
1 ½ tbsp. fresh lime juice

Process all ingredients in a food processor. Cover a baking sheet with parchment paper and place the mixture on top, pressing it down to cover the baking sheet. Chill for one hour.

Cut into bars and wrap separately. Store in refrigerator.

Sexy Black Rice Pudding

1 cup black rice, rinsed very well
1 cinnamon stick
3 ½ cups water
1 400-ml can of coconut milk
1/3 cup packed brown sugar

In a heavy medium saucepan, combine rice with the cinnamon stick and water and bring to a boil. Reduce heat to low and simmer, covered with a tight-fitting lid, for approx. 45 minutes.

Reserve ½ cup of coconut milk in a small bowl. Add the remaining milk and sugar to the rice. Cook, stirring frequently, until the sugar has dissolved and the mixture has thickened slightly, about 5 minutes.

Scoop rice into individual serving dishes and drizzle reserved milk over the pudding.

Yummy Muffins

1 cup buttermilk OR plain yogurt
2/3 cup packed brown sugar
¼ cup apple sauce
¼ cup canola or coconut oil
1 egg **or** 2 egg whites
2 tbsp. molasses

1 ½ cups natural bran
1 cup raisins
2/3 cup whole wheat flour
½ cup oats or wheat germ
¼ cup sesame seeds
¼ cup flax seeds
1 tsp. baking soda
½ tsp. salt
½ tsp. cinnamon

Preheat oven to 400°. Lightly grease a 12-muffin-cup pan; set aside.

In a large mixing bowl, whisk together the first six ingredients. Add the following nine ingredients and mix well.

Spoon the mixture into the muffin cups and bake for 15-20 minutes until golden brown or they spring back to touch. Remove from the pan and cool on a wire baking tray.

Your favourite recipes:

_____

_____

_____

_____

_____

_____

_____

_____

_____

_____

_____

_____

_____

_____

_____

_____

_____

Your favourite recipes:

_____

_____

_____

_____

_____

_____

_____

_____

_____

_____

_____

_____

_____

_____

_____

_____

_____

LIVING YOUR LIFE TO THE FULLEST

Imagine that you have won the following *PRIZE* in a contest:

Each morning your bank will deposit $86,400 into your private account for your use. However, this prize has rules:

1. Everything you don't spend during each day will be taken away from you.

2. You cannot simply transfer money into some other account.

3. You may only spend it.

4. Each morning, upon awakening, the bank opens your account with another $86,400 for that day.

5. The bank can end the game without warning; at any time, it can say, "Game Over!" It can close the account, and you will not receive a new one.

What would you personally do?

You would buy anything and everything you wanted, right? Not only for yourself but for all the people you love and care for. Even for people you don't know because you couldn't possibly spend it all on yourself, right?

You would try to spend every penny, and use it all, because you knew it would be replenished in the morning, right?

ACTUALLY…this GAME is REAL.

Each of us is already a winner of this *PRIZE*. We can't seem to see it.

The PRIZE is *TIME*

1. Each morning, we awaken to receive 86,400 seconds as a gift of life.

2. Any remaining time is not credited to us when we sleep at night.

3. What we haven't used up that day is forever lost.

4. Yesterday is forever gone.

5. The account is refilled each morning, but the bank can dissolve your account at any time WITHOUT WARNING...

So, what will YOU do with your 86,400 seconds?

Those seconds are worth so much more than the same amount in dollars. Think about it and remember to experience and enjoy every second of your life because time races by so much quicker than you think.

~Author Unknown~

Take care of yourself, be happy, love deeply, and enjoy life to the fullest! Experience each day as if it is your last. Here's wishing you a beautiful day. Start "spending."

"Inspiring Real Purpose and Real Change in the World"

MEET THE AUTHOR

As a highly accomplished national Fitness Presenter, an internationally recognized Yoga Instructor, a best-selling author, an Entrepreneur, a Life Coach, an Infinite Possibilities trainer, and a student of the Mind, Body & Spirit theory, Rhona Parsons "lights up" by guiding and instructing others to live their best life through fitness, health, and wellness.

Rhona has followed her love and passion for helping others by developing and teaching fitness, Pilates, and yoga programs for over two decades. She enjoys a successful fitness, health, and wellness career leading dynamic fitness, Yoga, and Pilates classes. Rhona has mentored many fitness and yoga instructors through instructor-training workshops.

As a body, mind, and spirit innovator, Rhona leads annual sold-out weekly Yoga Retreats in Mexico and Greece, where her clients get treated to five-star luxury. At the same time, they can relax, release, restore, and renew their body, mind, and spirit. Rhona is a caring, passionate person who loves her work. She is full of energy and a fun, caring, loving individual. Her dedication to her beliefs is always evident, and her ability to motivate clients through her vast knowledge is truly inspiring. Rhona is a clear, concise, and systematic instructor who inspires others to care for themselves and be kind to each other.

A mother of 3 amazing daughters and known as NanaRho to 8 incredible grandchildren, Rhona lives her truth by balancing her career, clients, and devotion to her family and their well-being.

Rhona offers a free 30-minute consultation to everyone looking for a new change in their life. You can reach her at:

Website: www.rhonaparsons.com
Email: rhona@rhonaparsons.com
Linked In: linkedin.com/in/rhona-parsons-3b534784
Facebook: https://www.facebook.com/vernonrhonaparsons

REFERENCES

Health Canada. Primary Food Nutrients. www.canada.ca/en/health-canada/services/nutrients.html

Harvard T. H. Chan School of Public Health, Boston. HIIT (High-Intensity Interval Training), www.hsph.harvard.edu/nutritionsource/high-intensity-interval-training

John Hopkins University. Target heart rate information. www.hopkinsmedicine.org/health/wellness-and-prevention/understanding-your-target-heart-rate

Mayo Clinic. www.mayoclinic.org/healthy-lifestyle/nutrition-and-healthy-eating/in-depth/water/art-20044256

Parsons, Rhona, "21 Ways to Bring Balance into Your Life", 2018

Peeke, Pamela, MD, MPH, FACP, "Body for Life for Women, Food portions 2005

Red Ventures, Fort Mills, South Carolina. RPE Scale, www.medicalnewstoday.com/articles/rate-of-perceived-exertion-rpe-scale-what-it-is-and-rate-of-perceived-exertion-rpe

St. Paul's Hospital, Vancouver, BC "Fibre Facts" and "Alcohol Facts," 2008

Torkos, Sherry, B. Sc. Phm. "The GI Made Simple", 2007

USADA, Colorado Springs, CO. www.usada.org/athletes/substances/nutrition/fluids-and-hydration/

Dotdash, Inc., New York, NY www.verywellfit.com. The three primary nutrients

www.heart.org/en/health-topics/high-blood-pressure/changes-you-can-make-to-manage-high-blood-pressure/how-potassium-can-help-control-high-blood-pressure

www.livestrong.com/article/362122-how-is-fat-stored-and-burned-as-energy-in-the-human-body

Made in the USA
Columbia, SC
04 June 2023

17508340R00126